Born To Win!

David Shearman

New Wine Press

New Wine Ministries
PO Box 17
Chichester
West Sussex
United Kingdom
PO19 2AW

Unless otherwise indicated, all Bible quotations are taken from The
Holy Bible, New International Version © Copyright 1973, 1978, 1984
International Bible Society. Published by Hodder & Stoughton.

ISBN 978-1-905991-29-7

Typeset by CRB Associates, Reepham, Norfolk
Printed in Malta

Contents

Foreword

All Christian believers start off with a fresh beginning, a new faith, an open future and a strong desire to be useful. Nobody wants to be a loser – but many Christians live in 'quiet desperation.'

As we grow older, we are aware of opportunities missed, and of life becoming more complex. There is no longer a 'job for life' guarantee; there is mixed joy and pain in marriage and parenting; financial pressures can be overwhelming; broken relationships devastating; and most importantly a catalogue of what may seem to be unanswered prayers.

The land that was once full of promise can at times appear to be bleak and even desolate. David Shearman understands all of this. Reading between the lines you can sense the scars of some tough battles on his personal pilgrimage. He has however, learnt to be a victor rather than a victim, and his journey is fascinating. Success is a **journey**, not a **destination**.

Drawing from scriptural stories he helps us to see our own pilgrimage in the light of God's love and grace, and realize the ability of the Holy Spirit to make you whole. With the barrage of pressures, temptations and responsibilities each of us face, becoming whole is one thing, staying whole is another.

David skillfully helps readers to find their way through the 'Do what seems right to you' philosophy that pervades society and leads people into both deception and trouble.

Jesus Christ is revealed as the ultimate winner. If we also desire to be winners there is a price to pay. The writer makes it clear that this is the only sensible way forward – it is the **only** journey we can take in the light of Calvary.

So take a break from your diary, reflect and refuel. Give God thanks that this man has become a victor who loves God, has battled through temptation and betrayal, has become enormously influential in his own and other nations, and is now seeking to reach out to those in pain – to those who feel they are losers.

If success is the ability to survive failure, then the author of this book is a success – indeed he is a winner!

Gerald Coates
May 1999

Introduction

You were born a winner. The struggle of sperm reaching egg in your mother's womb started your life as a winner. The much stated, and in some quarters hated comment, that the most un-safe place in the world is a mother's womb, means that when you were born you were continuing your winning ways.

Life takes its course and many people become victims in a multitude of ways, others triumph against amazing odds, but most live in mediocrity, never realizing their potential. God says in the Bible, that the things He has commanded us to do 'are not too difficult or beyond our reach.' In other words the 'you' who started life as a winner must learn some winning ways and thoughts. Whatever has happened to you cannot prevent you succeeding if only you learn to think as God thinks! The race of life is not so much a competition against others, but a challenge to become all you were born to be, to reach your potential and achieve your purpose. God has done everything necessary and provided all needed resources for you and me to win. There is no adequate excuse, everyone was Born to Win. Many who have gone before you have realized that with God's help they could succeed and God is as committed to your success as He has been to theirs.

Let me express this truth another way. God believes in designer starts and happy endings. I am not asking you to think about who your parents were, or where you were born, rather think that before the creation of the world, when God designed paradise, you were given a part in this plan. That's a designer start.

In a world so full of sad stories and unanswerable questions, is it realistic to also believe in happy endings? Somewhere inside most of us is a 'Happy ending longing' and I believe God is committed to finish the way He began. You were Born to Win, He gave you a designer start long ago and wants your co-operation for a happy ending in the future.

I invite you to take a journey with me through the pages of this book. I will share with you some of the secrets that are turning my life into a success. God says I was Born to Win, I am learning to believe and act on that truth. Will you? Let us be bold and begin our journey...

Chapter 1

Please Read Me a Story

'Book, book,' says two-year-old Chloe. 'Poppa' must read a story. Everyone loves a story, especially those human interest stories, where people overcome great odds, good triumphs over evil, and it ends 'happy ever after.' To start our journey, here is a story. Once upon a time...

My mother, I presume, was an orphan. I know she had been adopted by a couple, and when her foster-mother died, her foster-father began to sexually abuse her. She was only a teenager and so she ran away, but having nowhere to go and no one to turn to, she was forced to return home. I was conceived as a result of the continued abuse.

Finding herself pregnant, my mother applied to the Salvation Army for help, and was placed in a mothers and babies' home in Cardiff. I was born there in 1938. I stayed in this home for about a year before being transferred to the Church of England Children's Society. I was fostered to a succession of homes, eight in all, before I was seven years old. This was due partly to the contingencies of war, but by the end of this time my papers, for reasons I still don't know, were indelibly marked 'Not suitable for fostering'. My father died soon after I was born. I have no recollections of my mother.

In 1945, the foster parents with whom I had been living in Bath informed me suddenly that I was being moved to a children's home in Devon. There was no preparation, no explanation, and no farewell; just the threat that if I was not

a good boy, I would be locked up in a cupboard. I did not
look forward to living in Devon, but the day came when I
was put on a train in the care of the guard. Upon arrival at
Taunton station, the guard left me on a huge pile of crates
with a label around my neck. A short while later, a tall
figure strode down the platform whom I sensed had come
for me. He read the label, lifted me down, and without any
further introduction led me away to catch another train to a
village 15 miles distant. We alighted from the train and
walked a mile to the place I was to call home for the next
seven years.

On arrival, I was given a meal, but left most of it. Later,
at teatime, I was sitting at a long dining table when
someone shouted from the kitchen hatch, 'Who left their
lunch?' 'The new boy,' one of the lads called back. The
remains of my previous meal shortly replaced my tea. My
only possessions were the clothes I wore, a pencil, a new
notebook and a bag of liquorice allsorts. These were all
taken from me by the staff soon after I arrived. I never saw
them again, except for my clothes, which I later discovered
in a bag ready for disposal. Having been kitted out in the
home clothes, complete with second hand boots which
didn't fit, I was given the number 47, my new identity.
Finally I was shown the dormitory which I would share with
19 others.

The home was huge. It had been a prep school, but now
housed 120 boys. Supervision rather than interaction was
the order of the day. We were herded rather than cared for.
In such a large institution, mental, physical and even sexual
abuse was common. Most of the staff would have treated
animals better than they treated us.

Despite the number of boys in the home, it was a lonely
and friendless place. Friendship was not discouraged, but
the survival instinct dictated against it. Anyone you got
close to might be fostered at a moment's notice and leave
without warning or farewells. Nobody befriended me or
told me what to expect. I asked no questions, but watched
and listened, relying upon personal discovery to understand
the way the place was run. All this was part of the survival
instinct. In the course of time, I adapted to the regime and
saw many other boys arrive and then leave for foster
homes.

The first morning found me making my bed, turning the mattress, folding my bedclothes in a prescribed manner, and then running downstairs to wash and dress. All this had to be accomplished in ten minutes. If you had wet the bed you had to wash your sheets and peg them on the line in the playground. Occasionally I had to hang my sheets on the line and see them freeze stiff, all the time with no clothes on, and with the added penalty of sleeping on the floor. We were strongly discouraged from wetting the bed!

On Sundays we would walk, crocodile fashion, in our Sunday best, to attend church in the village. I guess we helped to swell the numbers. At the home, we were taught to recite our prayers, which confused me: 'God bless Mummy and Daddy, uncles and aunties and all kind friends, and make me a good boy, amen.' The only part that made any sense for most of us was the last phrase. This was the extent of our spiritual instruction.

After Sunday lunch, we would again march single file down the country lanes. If it was too wet to walk, we would write letters. Our notepaper was headed 'Waifs' and Strays' Society.' I often wondered if I was a waif or a stray, or perhaps both, and never understood why I still had to write to an imaginary mother, father, uncle or aunt.

All of us had a desire to know our roots – to answer the 'Who?' 'How?' and 'When?' questions. Some received responses to the letters they wrote; others were even visited by relatives. We talked about such things amongst ourselves, and discovered that all our details were kept in the office. Feeling very brave one day, I asked the headmaster – the 'gaffer' as we called him – if I had any relatives. He said he thought I had an uncle in Glamorgan, which I misunderstood, telling everyone I had an Uncle Morgan!

By the time I was 13, numbers at the home had dropped to 36, and I was renumbered 19. We all began to prepare for future change; a new gaffer and matron were coming. Before their formal appointment to the position, they were shown round the home. During their visit I heard them coming and hid under a table. I was seen and ordered to come out, whereupon the old gaffer pointed at me and said to the new man, 'See that boy? He's trouble; get rid of him.' I don't recall being violent, rebellious or naughty, and have no idea where this prejudice came from.

When the new couple arrived, we all noticed something different about them. For a start, they actually talked to us. I warmed to this, particularly when the gaffer promised to look into my family background. He talked a lot about God, but I was not interested, considering myself already a Christian; after all, I had been christened and confirmed, and I sang in the choir. I never had a problem in believing in God – I knew He was there, somewhere. From a sense of self-preservation, I held back from making any response. I was happy to enjoy the comfort of attention without the commitment of belief.

The new gaffer occasionally took us to Gospel meetings. While returning from one of these, the man driving the car asked if we were Christians; had we given our lives over to God? This left me confused. Was there something more I needed to do to become a Christian? When I asked the gaffer about it, he told me to find a Bible and look up John 3:16, substituting my name in the verse. I did this, and read that God so loved Michael, that He gave His only son. It struck home that God Himself loved **me** – one forsaken and unloved. I responded to this by asking Him to forgive my sin, and to make me His child.

This was the start of an incredible journey for me, and it hasn't finished yet. I realised that there was Someone who loved me, Someone I could trust. Space forbids me to tell you my full story and there are some things which I still have many questions about. The statement that *'In all things God works for the good of those who love Him'* (Romans 8:28) is no blithe platitude but one I have come to understand in greater fullness as my life has progressed.

At the home, life was still hard. I had grown deeply attached to this new gaffer, and when he said he was thinking of leaving, I cried day and night for a week at home and at school. No one asked why I was so upset – not that I would have told them anyway. I had been offered the chance to emigrate to Australia with a family, but I declined. In 1952 the home closed and we all had to decide where we wanted to go and live. I told the gaffer that I wanted to live with him and the matron. After a long while, permission was granted and I, of whom it had been written 'Not suitable for fostering,' had someone to call Mum and Dad.

We went to live in a real house in Exeter, where Mum lives to this day. I took a long time to adjust to this; the house seemed so small, and I had many problems knowing how to respond to love, having never been taught. My frustration vented itself in anti-social activities, particularly lying and stealing both in and out of my home. As a Christian I was ashamed of my double life, and once, while giving my testimony in a meeting, I heard the devil say 'Hypocrite!' I could not refute the condemnation and vowed to do something about my life. But what? I had tried before to stop, to no avail; stealing was both challenging and compulsive. Yet I kept secret lists of what I had stolen. I always intended to set things right.

One day, at a special meeting, the preacher seemed to be speaking directly to me. He said that God had the power to set people free from habits that enslaved them. At the end of the meeting I went forward and confessed my stealing for the first time, and someone prayed for me. The hard part came over the next few months, as I worked my way down my lists and paid for everything I had stolen. I later learnt that, had I not confessed, I would shortly have been discovered. I was glad I had responded to God and the action had come from me, rather than the law!

My last year of schooling was in Exeter. I was keen to share my faith, and would take tracts to school to give to some of the pupils. One incident that arose from this put the fear of God into me. There was a boy I shared a desk with who had a very filthy mind. Day after day he asked me for a tract until I finally gave in, though I knew he wasn't interested in its contents. Taking the tract, he gleefully ripped it into tiny shreds, threw them in the air and walked away laughing. A few months later he was up on the moors which were frequently used by the military. By chance he found an unexploded bomb which detonated when he picked it up, killing him instantly.

Several years later, I moved to Bristol and started working in the George Müller homes. Those massive granite buildings, the vision of one man inspired by God, had given shelter to so many orphans. Working in these homes was the start for me of a shift in my mind from **getting** to **giving**.

After a time, an opportunity arose for me in London, working in a hospital for children with skin problems. I enjoyed it there and found the job a great challenge, but my own health had begun to seriously deteriorate. I had been taught that God was a saving and a healing God, yet when I was taken into hospital needing major abdominal surgery, the heavens seemed as brass.

My faith in God was sorely tested; again rejection reared its ugly head. I came through the operation and made good progress, until one day complications arose and my life hung in the balance. Out of the depths I cried to God for comfort, and He spoke clearly to me: *'Your strength will equal your days'* (Deuteronomy 33:25). I knew instinctively that something had happened. I told the doctors I was on the mend, and within a few days I was able to eat and was soon well enough to be discharged.

In 1965 I moved to Nottingham. My foster parents were invited to open a boys' hostel there, and against normal procedure I was asked to become their deputy. I enjoyed the work and the challenge of the hostel. Most of the boys were 'problem' children from other homes, with similar backgrounds to my own. I was nearly always a step ahead of them! I found a local church, and very soon my attention was drawn to a young lady, the Pastor's daughter, who played the organ. I began to court her and within ten months of meeting we were married.

Thirty years later Ruth and I are still together, still in love with one another, and with two grown-up children who are a joy and a delight to us. The years have had their hard times, but God has been faithful to us and we've enjoyed a remarkably stable marriage. Ruth has been a tremendous help and support. More than anyone, she has helped me to come out of my shell of rejection. We both have responsibilities within and outside of our local church, we feel fulfilled and enjoy our ministry. I particularly enjoy the pastoral counselling of people within our community.

In spite of all the negatives from my birth onwards, I know my arrival in the world was no accident. God has a purpose for me that will not be thwarted. This review of the past confirms to me how good God is. He not only watched over my birth, but has kept me safe all my life. My prayer is that I should be of use to Him.

In the media, the delinquent behaviour of criminals is frequently excused or explained by reference to their background or upbringing. But we do not have to accept this belief that labels us merely 'victims' or 'survivors'. Consciously choosing to leave behind this useless victim paradigm, I know I can attain the purpose for which God made me. I have seen many things meant for my harm, being turned to my good. The knocks which life apportions can be used to change us from **victims** into **victors**. I have put my trust in the God who claims to be a Father to the fatherless. The lifting power of His redemption is stronger than all the downward forces of deprivation and delinquency.

The man described in this true story is a close friend of mine. Even as I write he has endured further difficulty, rushed to hospital last week. Even so, his spirit is strong and the power within him refuses to bow to the circumstances that would otherwise dominate his life.

'It's a nice story David, but it's not enough to help me.' Okay, let us press on with our journey and look at some other people; look for some clearer pictures. Like baby Chloe, we need another story.

Chapter 2

Just Another Story

'It's all right for you – you haven't had to go through the things I've suffered.' 'You don't understand; it's different for me.' Such comments are made daily by many people, and are the product of victim thinking where circumstances – anything or anyone – are blamed for a person's past or present state of mind and actions. This paradigm, usually much more subtle than expressed above, limits the potential of millions.

Sitting in a comfortable restaurant run by nuns in Bobo, Burkina Faso, I was fascinated by the story of a successful businessman who had broken free from a life of drudgery. Brought up in unrelenting poverty, he worked hard and applied himself to obtain a good education. He travelled to Europe for further study and now runs one of the biggest factories in the second city of this West African state. In my travels around the world I have met many similar people – men and women who have broken out of the poverty cycle and attained success, where continuing poverty would have been the normal course of events. By poverty I mean something much more than gross economic hardship.

Some time ago a boy was born in circumstances we might objectively describe as 'unfavourable'. His parents were not married, and were travelling at the time of his birth. Dangerous events in their own country, occupied as it was by a foreign military power, made it prudent for them to live as immigrants abroad. When political change came, the little family were able to return to their home country and resume a normal life. The boy grew up in a town of dubious repute. His father ran a small family business and the boy's obvious gifts and talents were not encouraged or developed. Brothers and sisters were later born to his parents. As a case history analyzed by the Social Services of most Western democracies, there would be an expectation of the boy to exhibit antisocial behaviour. The psychological problems associated with illegitimacy, lack of suitable medical help at the time of birth, refugee status, and the political ruthlessness surrounding his early years, could easily lead to insecurity, vulnerability and rejection. The restriction of creativity during adolescence would almost certainly give rise to further frustration. Combined, these facets of this boy's early life would be sufficient to provoke a case of delinquency, but the teenager in our story at no time behaved as a delinquent.

Leaving his parental home when about thirty years old, life might have become easier – a different town, more opportunities, a new start. However, living as a displaced person he was frequently misrepresented, was often in conflict with the authorities, and had substantial reason to develop serious paranoia. Things came to a head within a few years. The victim of political intrigue, he was arrested under false pretences, was beaten up by soldiers of the army occupying his homeland, and suffered a mock trial at which he was sentenced to death by torture. After the circumstances he had endured as a young child, a man whose life culminated with such an amount of emotional pressure, injustice and misunderstanding might be expected to be surly, angry, aggressive, or self-assertive. At no time did the subject of our story show such characteristics.

The man I have described above with some poetic license is Jesus Christ. This is how the Bible relates His attitude to the unjust punishment before His death:

> *'He was oppressed and afflicted, yet He did not open His mouth; He was led like a lamb to the slaughter, and as a sheep before her shearers is silent, so He did not open His mouth.'* (Isaiah 53:7)

If any man ever had reason to be trapped by victim thinking, blame His circumstances and the failure of others, Jesus Christ did, but He never gave way to the pressure of circumstances. He lived as a man filled with a power that made Him a victor rather than a victim, a success instead of a slave.

His story doesn't end where we left it. Having been killed, He came back to life and was seen by many hundreds of people. He is still alive, the daily friend and companion of millions of people the world over. The power that raised Him from the dead made the difference for my friend Mike and the African businessman whose stories I told earlier. They welcomed Jesus Christ to take charge of their lives while living as victims. Jesus Christ makes all the difference. It can be the same for you and me.

I was born into a loving family. Although we moved around to live in various parts of England and Northern Ireland, our home was stable. My mother was a great homemaker given to kindness and hospitality, and my father a busy minister. Together, they gave my brother and me an excellent example and a solid start in life. That is my simple story, but millions of people do not share the same stable start. As you read on, your mind may be flooded with thankfulness for a good home. If so, please be truly grateful. On the other hand, you may be filled with painful memories, some of which you may have attempted to keep from surfacing.

Some people are born into *de facto* families which, though stable, do not enjoy the commitment of marriage. Many such relationships, including marriages, are not stable; the statistics illustrate an increasing nightmare. It is reasonable that every child should know the security of two parents, each contributing their separate and combined skills to the home, as man and woman, father and mother. Millions of people are denied such a privilege. Many live fatherless, a situation which has huge social implications. With inadequate male role models, how should young boys establish their masculinity? The answer is often manifested through aggression and sexual conquest. Similarly, fatherless girls have no-one to display the loving, caring side of manhood; many of these young victims grow to maturity with a jaundiced view of the aggressive, self-seeking male who must always be viewed with suspicion. More desperately, other children are not simply denied loving mother and father figures, but are used and abused as objects for another person's pleasure.

I immediately think of some of the people I have met: the urchins of Smoky Mountain – the main rubbish tip in Manila; the street children of Guatemala city; Mary, a young girl living in disused squat accommodation with an alcoholic mother, who would often wake to find yet another man in the family bed. I think of Bob, a bubbly Londoner who was ferrying guns for the London underworld before the age of ten. His spiral downwards stopped when he was rescued, destitute and drinking metal polish, by the Salvation Army. At the other end of this spectrum are some of the Designer Children who live in plenty, wanting for nothing, but brought up largely by a nanny followed by a boarding school and arriving in adulthood very short on love.

I do not seek to add words to a known social problem. Rather, I wish to state that all adults and children who have been victims of an unsatisfactory start in life can live without being emotional wrecks, blaming past circumstances or present inabilities, and can rise above being stoic survivors who are making the best of a bad job. The example of Jesus Christ gives every child the chance. Whether still young or now mature, whether blessed with many things, or denied all security, or even desperate from life's injustice, each of us was born to win. It was not true that Jesus was a bastard, but many people called Him one. It was not true that His step-father Joseph did not care about His birth, but many did not understand. The unusual start to His life didn't knock Him off course. He knew He was special. So are you. If, like Mary and Bob who I mentioned above, you allow the same life force that motivated Jesus to live in you, you can break out of victim thinking, blaming the circumstances, and always crying, 'You don't understand!' or, 'Get me out of here!'

To be born in this present world makes you a survivor. It is a deplorable statistic that one of the most dangerous places in the modern world is a mother's womb. A friend of mine was teaching a class of school children about the horrors of the Third Reich. He told them of the major moral, ethical and political errors of that awful regime, and made mention of the hundreds of thousands of people who gave their lives to overthrow the evil of that time on the battlefields of the second world war. These are well-known facts, but few people are aware of how clearly abortion and euthanasia were part of Hitler's eugenics agenda in his quest for a race of Aryan supermen, of which the mass murder of Jews is the best known part. Policies which people died to prevent fifty years ago are now enshrined in the laws of the nations that fought Hitler. Public discussion regarding euthanasia in the mass media is approached from supposed humanitarian grounds. The ethical considerations of embryo screening for disease, deformity or handicap, with a view to subsequent abortion, are swept under the carpet in the fanfare of this scientific breakthrough.

The problems have been around for so long we could be forgiven for thinking, 'This is the way things are meant to be.' Despite moral and political claims, nobody is truly fit to lead us into an improved quality of living. Most have some bad habits they cannot (or do not want to) control. The problems of social inequality have always been with us; criminal fallout is a fact of life. But is this the end of the matter? The answer is both yes and no. True, there are many problems in every part of the world, both with individuals and societies, but this need not be the way that we, as individuals, communities and societies, should remain or were intended to live.

If we were designed to be successes, not just survivors, let alone slaves, what must we do to change our thoughts, words and actions? How can we achieve a nature change? Freud's psychoanalytic concept of the *id*, – the deepest part of the subconscious, devoted entirely to pleasure in the most self-serving manner and driven by blind impulse – is so unhelpful it leaves me cold. Is our deepest desire nothing beyond a profoundly base, selfish pleasure, pandering to animal instincts? We need a better pattern to aspire to without which things can never improve. The Christian view agrees that everyone has become a slave and a victim; slaves to doing, saying and thinking wrong – the Bible calls it sin – and victims of the consequences of our individual and collective behaviour. But it also insists that we were designed for something better, and offers us power to live differently.

I have introduced the language of **slave**, **survivor** or **success** – highly emotive words. I need to tell you another story, a very old one, to illustrate these words. It is a fascinating tale that will probably challenge us to review the way we live and think. We may not like that challenge, and we can protect ourselves by thinking, 'It's only a story' – but be warned, this story may bite back!

Chapter 3

Once Upon a Time

A long time ago, a unique family who, with the passage of millennia, have become today's State of Israel, went on a journey. A wealthy family in a difficult economic climate, they decided to explore the opportunities offered by a neighbouring country, and chose to emigrate. The root cause of this upheaval was not the economic pressure the family was under, but was triggered by a strange episode some twenty plus years prior to the move itself. One member of the family – a son named Joseph, presumed dead by his father Jacob, but actually sold as a slave by his brothers – had been brought to live in Egypt, the neighbouring 'land of opportunity'. After a remarkable series of happenings, Joseph found himself in a position of considerable power and influence in the government, and following some bizarre but moving events, his father also came to live in Egypt and the two were reunited. Due to his position as Prime Minister of all Egypt, Joseph was able to arrange things very favourably for his family, and they prospered. Their population increased dramatically.

Nearly 400 years later, none of Jacob's descendants had any experiential knowledge of how good life was in the days of their forebears. (Have you any idea of what life was like in your family 400 years ago?) From the relative ease their ancestors had enjoyed, the winds of change had blown against them, and their host country was oppressing them. Political expediency dictated against them, and daily life became a grind. The people no longer worked out of choice, but were forced into slavery. Driven by taskmasters, they had no trade unions, no rights, and no tea breaks; nothing but higher production demands. This work force probably helped to build some of the great pyramids of Egypt. Nobody in the whole community knew what it was like to be a free person. After ten generations of this treatment, none of them remembered the favoured times when one of their relatives was Prime Minister.

The concept of slavery is not confined to physical or geographic limitation. Mental and social barriers imprison millions in slavery mindsets. Tens of thousands of young people congregate in the centre of the City of Nottingham, where I live, each Friday and Saturday night. Eating, drinking, looking for pleasure, spending their money; they would talk about 'having a good time'. But speak to many of them after the weekend, when all their money is spent, their dreams are unfulfilled and they are nursing a hangover, and they would probably agree that life must offer some more rewarding alternatives. Remarkable as it may seem, most of them will be doing the same semi-fulfilling thing next week, with the same result! Call it the herd instinct or talk of following the line of least resistance – in essence it is slavery to a habit pattern, conformity to an expected or accepted norm in society.

But what were we truly designed for? Have we been slaves in one way or another for so long that nobody can remember how good life should be? A deliverer came for the ancient Israelites in the shape of a man named Moses. Their circumstances changed and they were able to escape from their slavery. Let us investigate. We may find some contemporary answers.

Moses was eighty years old when God called him to his destiny, and his initial response was: *'I am not the person for a job like that!'* (Exodus 3:11, The Living Bible). He was on Egypt's 'most wanted' list subsequent to an abortive attempt at saving the Israelites forty years previously. Reluctantly obedient to God's commissioning orders, he convinced the leaders of the slave community of his authenticity and then set himself to the daunting task of emancipating his nation from its 400–year-long nightmare.

The Israelites were a continual trouble to the Egyptians, but as slaves they were also an enormous economic benefit. The political landscape would change significantly if they were not available, so the Egyptians had no intention of letting them leave. With Moses on the scene, conditions were ripe for a big struggle. Moses and his eloquent brother Aaron went and told the king of Egypt, *'Let the people go'* – the cry of many a slave nation. You might think them naïve, for the immediate result was predictable:

> *'The King of Egypt said, "Moses and Aaron, why are you taking the people away from their labour? Get back to your work!" ... That same day Pharaoh gave this order to the slave drivers and foremen in charge of the people: "You are no longer to supply the people with straw for making bricks; let them go and gather their own straw. But require them to make the same number of bricks as before; don't reduce the quota." '*   (Exodus 5:6–8)

As with many of life's changes, things often become worse before they become better. It is always darkest just before dawn, the saying goes, but many people refuse to press through the pain barrier to arrive at a better day. Moses had another meeting with God in which he expressed these same sentiments.

> *'Ever since I went to Pharaoh to speak in your name, he has brought trouble upon this people, and you have not rescued your people at all.'*   (Exodus 5:23)

Moses, a good leader, was at that unenviable position in a series of events when the end is not yet in sight, and the benefits are not visible. He was nervous, he needed reassurance, and so God (who knew the situation exactly) spoke to him.

> *'I will bring you out from under the yoke of the Egyptians. I will free you from being slaves to them, and I will redeem you ... I will take you as my own people, and I will be your*

God ... I will bring you to the land I swore with uplifted hand to give ... [Signed] I am the LORD.' (Exodus 6:6–8)

Moses received his full assignment as the herald of God's judgement against Egypt and its king, which came in the form of ten plagues. How would this translate to the modern world? Britain suffered freak winds in October 1987 damaging the economy; Japan has suffered earthquakes and related disasters; monsoon floods in India, and the horror of famine and drought in East Africa are at the zenith of this escalating scale. All these events have taken their toll. The cost in lives, energy, hope and money is incalculable. Egypt must have been devastated after its ten plagues.

After the disastrous final night of judgement, with death all around him and everyone else in Egypt, Pharaoh wanted Moses' people to leave. The Egyptians drove the Israelites out, laden with the wealth of Egypt, just as God had said they would. In one night, 400 years of tyranny were over, and the Israelites were no longer slaves, controlled by the will of others. This was a turning point in their history. Nothing would ever be the same again. They were pilgrims once more, as their forefathers had been, moving forward.

The change was more than geographical as the Israelites moved from Egypt into the wilderness. Their thinking changed from, 'Get me out of here!' (although they occasionally fell to eulogising their life in Egypt), and developed into 'Please' and 'Thank you' for the expected provision of their daily needs. The biblical account shows God Himself as their butcher, baker and candlestick maker, not to mention their tailor and cobbler. After the unremitting slavery of former times, life had suddenly become very comfortable. Everything was provided for them: food, water, warmth, light, shade. All their needs were met.

How many people living in the affluent parts of the world have most (if not all) of their needs met? Sufficient money to buy all the food and clothes needed, clean water out of the tap, quick and convenient transport, and help available for every conceivable crisis situation. Life has become easy. Unfortunately, like the Israelites, we lapse into presumption rather than remaining grateful. Reflecting on conditions (in the West) during both the nineteenth and the war-torn twentieth centuries, we should be thankful for our many blessings; instead, we expect them – they are regarded as a prerogative. The millennia have passed, but the human race has learned remarkably little.

In the relative paradise the Israelites were now experiencing, they had forgotten their heritage; they were pilgrims. Their slavery was behind them, but they were still only living in day-to-day survival; they should have been aiming for a better place – their Promised Land. Why, with all the material blessings of modern living, are there so many unfulfilled and empty people with broken homes and broken lives? Why so many suicides? Why so many drug-dependent, hopeless young people, while 'Mr and Mrs Average' pass through grey lives knowing deep inside that there must be more to live for?

Could it be that we have forgotten to be pilgrims, especially in the spiritual dimension of our humanity? Many live an emaciated spiritual life, only glimpsing the spiritual world through the tarot card, the horoscope and fortune teller, or on some drug trip, never enjoying the positive spiritual nourishment available through a personal relationship with their Creator. While surviving quite happily, the ancient people we are observing knew, both from their tribal history and from Moses informing them, that the future was beckoning them on to a very different life.

They sent some spies ahead to explore the possibilities. After forty days of exploration and bringing samples of the fruit of the land with them, they returned to report:

> 'We went into the land to which you sent us and it does flow
> with milk and honey! Here is its fruit. But the people who
> live there are powerful, and the cities are fortified and very
> large. We even saw descendants of Anak there.'
>
> (Numbers 13:27, 28)

The reporter must have sounded nervous, for Caleb (who was rather an enthusiast) added:

> 'We should go up and take possession of the land, for we can certainly do it.'

However, the fearful majority said:

> ' "We can't attack those people; they are stronger than we are." And they spread a bad report among the Israelites ... "The land we explored devours those living in it. All the people we saw there are of great size. [What a contradiction!] We seemed like grasshoppers in our own eyes, and we looked the same to them." ' [What a declaration!]
>
> (Numbers 13:31, 33)

God had promised the land to them, He had proved Himself in the amazing deliverance from the Egyptians, but through their 'grasshopper' attitude they were robbed of their future and subjected to wandering for forty years in the desert. Only Caleb, Joshua and the younger people lived to see the land that had been promised to the whole community when they came out of Egypt. In the fullness of time, they subdued and possessed it, as had been promised. But how many people who should have enjoyed the experience, missed out, content to live in **survival** rather than the **success** of the Promised Land?

What can we learn from all this? Our time will certainly come and our promises will be fulfilled, but only if we are daring and prepared to try something new. 500 years ago, Columbus took the risk of disaster, ignominy and death and discovered the New World. Why should it be the next generation in your family, your business, your church, your town or your country to break out of survival into success? Why not you, now? Break out of past limitation, past failure or past slavery and possess **your promised land**. Don't stay with the doubters, trudging round in circles waiting to die, holding on to yesterday's stories. Leave the grasshopper paradigm behind. How do you know what others think about you anyway? The Israelites' later found out that their enemies had heard about their dramatic departure from

Egypt, and were themselves terrified. You were made to be neither a slave nor a survivor, but a success, achieving your very best. Are you reading the story of your life incorrectly? You were born to win.

'Again Poppa, again' and so the story must be read again. That is enough excuse for me to tell the Jesus story once more before we venture any further on our pilgrimage.

Chapter 4

Tell Me the Story Again

'*In the beginning*' are the opening words of the Bible. In this beginning, man is identified as being created in God's image and likeness with authority to manage the rest of creation, in a place of honour, freewill, self-control and purpose. Cross the millennia and look at mankind today. Many wars are being fought between various nations of the world. The North is holding the South to ransom in the tight grip of interest repayments. The rich of the world are throwing away more than the poor ever see or taste. Many do not have enough to eat, but there is always money for guns. Rumours are rife of aid from donor countries finding its way to fuel wars that United Nations soldiers are unable to prevent.

Not all is doom and gloom; sometimes a tide of generosity flows against the awful tide of injustice, selfishness and unacceptable behaviour, with individuals, groups, agencies and sometimes even nations showing the better face of humanity. Since the designer start of 'the beginning', many different people have lived, affecting the history of our world in many different ways, for good or bad. By any reckoning, Jesus Christ is the exceptional contributor to the history of mankind. A much-quoted but anonymous essayist wrote of Him:

> 'Nineteen long centuries have come and gone, and today He is the centrepiece of the human race and the

leader of the column of progress. I am far within the mark when I say that all the armies that ever marched, all the navies that ever were built, all the parliaments that ever sat and all the kings that ever reigned, put together, have not affected the life of man upon this earth as powerfully as has that one solitary life.'

The Christian Gospel declares Jesus Christ to be God, but also insists that He took on complete humanity, being born into this world with the Virgin Mary as His mother. Despite being God, He lived on earth as a man, laying aside all the rights and advantages due to His divine nature, yet living filled with God's power. The Apostle Paul recognised Him as the link between Adam and us when he declared:

'For as in Adam all die, so in Christ all will be made alive.'
(1 Corinthians 15:22)

If humanity is to have any hope of returning to its original purpose or attaining its full future worth, Jesus Christ is the key figure around whom necessary changes must be effected. He triumphed over every barrier to the fulfilment of His purpose. He offers us a pattern to escape from our victim lives; with the escape comes the potential for a better society.

The genocide in Rwanda in the mid-1990s has left many children orphaned, mutilated and confused. Jesus found Himself living in another country because of the barbaric, infanticidal practices of the political leadership of His home nation. Jesus may have been too young to be affected by the sights and sounds of such awful events, but escaping to live in another culture must have had an impact on Him. Though pressured though His early life, He manifestly remained undamaged by His experiences. To any of us who carry the wounds of displacement, racial hatred or insecurity in unfamiliar surroundings, He offers the power to break free. We need not remain victims of childhood wounds, but can choose to be enriched and made emotionally whole as He lives His life through us and we live out our lives in His strength.

In the course of time, Jesus' family returned to the land of Judea and settled in Nazareth. Being devout, they made the great religious pilgrimages required of them under Jewish law. During one such excursion Jesus' parents lost Him. After a three day search they found Him in the temple courts:

> *'Sitting among the teachers, listening to them and asking them questions. Everyone who heard Him was amazed at His understanding and His answers.'*   (Luke 2:46–47)

His parents were astonished. I wonder whether, crisis over, His mother over-reacted; who knows? I don't know what tone of voice she used, but she could almost be scolding Him:

> *'Son, why have you treated us like this? Your father and I have been anxiously searching for you.'*   (Luke 2:48)

I appreciate her concern. But notice Jesus' reaction to her question; He chooses to answer positively and respectfully to His parents thereby defusing the problem entirely, instead of asserting His rights, His position and His identity:

> *' "Why were you searching for me? Didn't you know I had to be in my father's house?" But they did not understand what He was saying to them. Then He went down to Nazareth with them and was obedient to them. And Jesus grew in wisdom and stature, and in favour with God and men.'*
> (Luke 2:49–52)

As a young man, Daley Thompson was always getting into trouble until someone saw his potential. His immense talent and frustrated creativity were fully focused as he took the gold medal for the Decathlon in the 1980 and 1984 Olympics, becoming a star athlete. All that is known about Jesus is that He grew in stature, as every normal young man does. There are no biblical records of any noteworthy events for a further 18 years. Unlike Daley Thompson, Jesus' potential was not released – social scientists might speak of His repressed creativity, with few opportunities for personal improvement, but He did not let this turn Him sour.

As a consequence of moving from Northern Ireland to England as a boy, I missed a good educational opportunity. How should I react? I took time to come to terms with it, but I believe that all things have worked together for my good. I refuse to be a victim of my circumstances. Jesus offers us all the power to break out of victim thinking and become victorious. Whatever the circumstances of your life, Jesus has been there already, and He came out as a victor, not a victim. You were not born to be dominated by circumstances, however frustrating or difficult, you were born to win, conquering limitation and deficiency.

Jesus' life moved on. After humbling Himself to the baptism that John was practising by the River Jordan, He enjoyed an amazing experience when the Holy Spirit descended on Him in the form of a dove. His testing in the wilderness followed this remarkable event. Luke, a first-century doctor, next describes the religious ceremony at the Nazareth synagogue when Jesus reads a 700-year-old prophecy made by Isaiah, and makes a staggering application of it to himself, saying, *'Today this scripture is fulfilled in your hearing'* (Luke 4:21). But the people took offence at His claim, and after a few sharp comments drove Him out of town. It would be easy to get the feeling that you are not very welcome. 'Don't rock our religious boat; go away!'

After some prefatory remarks, the Apostle John introduces the public part of Jesus' life with a story about a wedding. Jesus seemed to enjoy doing good things in the context of food and drink. The gospel story is full of similar fascinating incidents. Such thoughts of enjoyment did not please the legalistic Pharisees. Nothing's changed. In the twentieth century, there are those who still take offence at the idea of Jesus enjoying life. People were enthralled and captivated by Jesus' lively company at a dinner party, yet at these times He was also misrepresented and attacked, and attempts were made to trick Him. Humanity still greets Him with such a mixed response.

Having raised His friend Lazarus from the dead, things reached new extremes. Lazarus' family were overjoyed and many who had seen the miracle turned to believe in Jesus, but the chief priests and the ruling party felt very differently and called a meeting of their supreme court. They viewed the situation as a power struggle, and hated Jesus for it:

> ' *"What are we accomplishing?" they asked. "Here is this man performing many miraculous signs. If we let Him go on like this, everyone will believe in Him, and then the Romans will come and take away both our place and our nation."*
>
> (John 12:47–48)

You may have been misrepresented. People love and hate you at the same time. All emotions and attitudes can be found around us, and sometimes show themselves in us. Jesus never lost His temper – even when He was legitimately angry. He never spoke out of place, defended Himself, or became aggressive or vindictive when His enemies attacked. It is His life living through you and your life lived in His strength that will make the difference, break the cycle and change the way you think, act and speak. We were not born to be dominated by circumstances or uncontrolled emotions, for if the man Jesus could succeed against such ferocious odds, with His help, we can too.

Whatever the circumstances of our birth, childhood or development, whatever disappointment, misrepresentation or hatred we have endured, we can turn them all to make them work for us. Jesus' victorious life was measured in the greatest test of all. He could have let himself become paranoid about the people who were trying to kill Him, as they often were. He was betrayed, and after a mock trial He was subjected to disgusting and barbarous brutality. The scourging He suffered would have left Him with no flesh on His back; a crown of long thorns was forced onto His head; His face was pummelled by His captors, leaving Him virtually unrecognisable. Finally, He was sentenced to a torturous death by crucifixion.

He was deserted by many of His followers and, worst of all, deserted by God. *'My God, my God, why have you forsaken me?'* the Psalmist had prophetically cried in words that Jesus echoed from the cross (Psalm 22:1; Mark 15:34). He became sin on our behalf, and so cleared the offending rebellion against God that was at the root of all mankind's problems. Yet still in His dying agony, physically, emotionally and spiritually tormented, He had words of comfort and life for a criminal crucified alongside Him who pleaded:

> ' *"Jesus, remember me when you come into your Kingdom."* *Jesus answered him, "I tell you the truth, today you will be* *with me in paradise." '*   (Luke 23:42, 43)

Then He committed His Spirit into His Father's care, and died. I stand amazed at this. Throughout His life, with all the injustice and pain, there was never a wrong thought or word. No anger, no threats, no loss of composure; only a profound equanimity, calmness and compassion.

I remember being deeply touched as a boy sitting at our family meal table listening to Teddy Hodson, a missionary, telling wonderful stories of his life in Central Africa. Very shortly afterwards we heard that he had been hacked to death with machetes during an uprising. 'Faithful unto death' has been the prescribed line for many of Jesus' followers. I do not ask for it myself, but the truth remains that if He could triumph against such appalling injustice and inhuman treatment, He can help us through every test – the ones we are still scarred from, and those we have yet to face. Letting Him live out His life through us, and living our lives in His strength, we need never be victims or slaves to our circumstances. Even in death He triumphed! You and I were born to win, not to live blaming the betrayal of others, the mistreatment, injustice or other prejudice we may have suffered. We need not be victims but victors, not survivors but successful people, first on the inside and then in the world around our lives.

The history of the Israelites and the life of Jesus are two pictures I have used to illustrate the human pilgrimage. Jesus succeeded in His purpose, losing neither His dignity, His self-control nor His focus, while completely fulfilling that which He came to earth to achieve. In reviewing the Israelites' story, we need to honestly assess our own lives. Are we still slaves in any way? Worst of all, are we slaves to sin? Do we lack the control, power and ability to be what we know we want to be? Like the slaves in Egypt, are we accepting suffering as an inevitable part of normal life? God sent Moses as a deliverer for them; He has sent a deliverer to us also. Jesus Christ died to break the controlling power of sin-slavery, and then rose again. If you ask Him, He will help you, He will give you His successful resurrection life. You will be empowered to live a new life in a different way with His strength.

If the story of Jesus seems out of your reach and the ancient history of Israel is too remote, I trust the human-interest stories of my contemporaries and my own honest pilgrimage will encourage you to continue on the journey. Stopping is not the best answer. Catch your breath for a few paragraphs as I challenge my 'Christian' readers, for we (I include myself) may need to break new ground on our journey.

Many Christians know the power of salvation, yet are still trapped in victim thinking and blame-shifting. Past circumstances or other people are used in attempts to excuse and justify wrong behaviour. Remember, whatever has happened to us has already happened to Jesus. He was always a victor. Be honest, recognise your weaknesses and ask Jesus to help you. He will give you the necessary power to change the way you think and live. Next, I ask myself 'Am I, in any way, a survival thinker?' Survival is much more comfortable than slavery, but the comparison can give a false impression. It may be better, but it is not where we are meant to stay; the wilderness is not the place of arrival. Neither is it a place requiring great faith. Jesus came out of His wilderness in the power of God's Spirit, and so must we.

Do we live as the Israelites did, apparently dependent on God, but more dependent on our leaders? If the water was bitter, if they didn't have what they wanted or thought that they should have, they immediately blamed Moses and Aaron, their leaders. They were not fully mature and would not take full responsibility for their lives. In the relative comfort and safety of the desert, there were no giants to kill, no ground to break with hard work, no seed to sow, and none of the promised milk-and-honey living. The wilderness was a glorified social welfare programme. Everything was provided, and everyone had cradle-to-grave protection, but this engendered a 'needs-met' survival paradigm; preferable to slavery, but not the best. They were tenants, not owners; consumers, not providers; living reactive and not pro-active lives.

Observation shows that much of the Christian church lives this way. So many neat little Christian families living comfortably with the bills all paid, everyone healthy, holidays to look forward to. 'We don't need anyone else. You gather your food and we'll gather ours.' Have we forgotten that we are pilgrims? We have promises and we are on a mission – a journey with a purpose. This Gospel of the Kingdom must be preached in the entire world, that:

> 'Through the church, the manifold wisdom of God should be made known to the rulers and authorities in the heavenly realms.'   (Ephesians 3:10)

In short, we must go where we have never been before.

The clear message from Moses to the children of Israel was, 'Don't be content with survival; stay as pilgrims, and don't stop until you have inherited the Promised Land.' The clear message from the life of Jesus to us is that whatever problems we might have, we need not continue living as victims or as slaves. He has been through the pain, and has conquered all emotional damage. He lived to give, not to get; to bless and not to blame; to shine as a light, not to hide in the darkness; never making excuses, but taking responsibility; always a victor, never a victim. The friend whose story I told at the beginning of the book took the strength that Jesus' life offers and so can you, whatever your past. Change your thinking. With Him living out His life through you, you too can conquer your circumstances and be a victor, for you were born to win.

Having established where we should live and whose power and strength we need to live there, let us press on with our journey. How do we do it? What principles will take us to Promised Land Living? Jesus offers us a pattern and power for living which is radically different from the alternatives on the human solution menu. My own journey, now many years long, has brought some things into sharper focus. These are the principles I share with you in the following chapters. I am still on the pathway. It is a pilgrimage and we may become tired on the way, but come, let us press on.

> There must be a beginning of any great matter, but the continuing unto the end, until it be thoroughly finished, yields the true glory.   (Attributed to Sir Francis Drake)

Chapter 5

Now is the Time

In our review of ancient history we saw how, once the Israelites had left Egypt and received their unique legal system at Mount Sinai, they poised themselves to enter the land of Canaan which God had promised them. Yet having made the start away from slavery and domination, on through survival and dependence, they stopped in the middle of their pilgrimage. The three opening verses of the book of Deuteronomy indicate what a long stop it was:

> 'It takes eleven days to go from Horeb to Kadesh Barnea by the Mount Seir road. In the fortieth year [after leaving Egypt] ... Moses proclaimed to the Israelites all that the Lord had commanded him concerning them.'
>
> (Deuteronomy 1:2)

All that separated the Israelites from their redemption from slavery and the borders of the Promised Land was an eleven-day journey. It took them forty years to complete it! The poignancy in the text is remarkable, separating the two statements with one full stop. The Israelites spent the gap between these two statements wandering around the Sinai desert.

Do you know anyone – let us include ourselves in this examination – who has spent days, weeks, months or years going round such a full stop? Opportunities lost, the days of our lives wasted. Thinkers down the ages have recognised the value of time as an asset, distributed in equal measure to all, and in different measure only according to the number of our days. Virgil's pithy observation *'tempus fugit'* (time flies) is a common phrase. 'Procrastination is the thief of time' is a common English aphorism which has been matched by the reflection that procrastination is not merely the thief of time, but is also the grave of opportunity. 'Be wise today, 'tis madness to defer. While we're talking, envious time is fleeing – seize the day [*carpe diem*]' counselled Horace in the first century BC. On a more sombre note, consider the last words attributed to Queen Elizabeth I:

'All my possessions for a moment of time.'

Against the air of desperation carried in these sayings, the Bible brings a degree of balance.

'There is a time for everything, and a season for every activity under heaven.' (Ecclesiastes 3:1)

The words of Jesus Christ have a more demanding bite:

'No procrastination. No backward looks. You can't put God's kingdom off till tomorrow. Seize the day.'
(Luke 9:62, *The Message*)

The good and the great have spoken, but each of us must heed the warnings and respond to their advice on our own account. Now is the time, today is the day. Time and opportunity wait for no man.

I said to a group of students I was teaching recently, 'This is the only Wednesday we get this week, so we may as well enjoy it.' Some seemed to like the idea, others found it too much to take in. The practical principle I was seeking to highlight was personal self-discipline, to which there are no short cuts. Whatever your personality, be active in thinking positively, and advance towards your life rather than taking a passive, entirely reflective stance. This approach will both lengthen the sunny, happy days and will shorten and give you strength to endure and learn from the sad or difficult ones. Whatever is happening, make the most of every opportunity, put your gifts to work, and use time to add experiences to your memory, the library of your imagination.

Viewing the use of time from a Christian perspective requires some mature judgement. On the one hand, God knows the end from the beginning. He is in complete control, and has mapped out our lives. The extreme (and somewhat fatalistic) conclusion here is that we must simply accept what comes to us. At the other extreme, God has given us freedom of choice, desire and will. He invites us to use these attributes to love Him and desire what He wants for us, and to so attain fulfilled lives at the pinnacle of His created order, made in His image and likeness. Thus a part of our existence seems passive and accepting, while another part requires an active and decisive attitude. Only with experience and a teachable and humble spirit can we learn to discern when each part is appropriate. But if we are to make mistakes, let us err on the side of action: it is much easier to steer a moving vehicle than push a stationary one. Life is directed by the choices we make. 'Life is a decision,' a friend of mine has often said. We live by our choices. Whatever you have been in the past, decide to be decisive from today!

People's lives are limited by a compass of compromise, indecision, previous thought patterns and lack of vision. If any of these words strike home and resonate uncomfortably in you, make a choice to change things. Now is the time to decide, and the choice will never be any easier. 'Whatever God wants' is a standard Christian excuse for inactivity and indecision – beware of it! Christians and non-Christians alike have an array of excuses, most of them a camouflage for laziness or fear, all of which limit the horizons of our lives and stop us reaching our promised land. The principle is summarised in ten very powerful two-letter words in the English language:

'If it is to be, it is up to me.'

'It's all too slick. "Make it happen! Be decisive!" It sounds like a sales' manager's pep talk', some might protest. If these ideas are taken to an extreme position and not viewed parallel with some of the other aspects of life, I would agree. But the truth remains in the face of overstatement: most people need to be more decisive and active in the choices and opportunities life brings their way.

In the *précis* of Israelite history presented earlier, I mentioned Joseph, one of my favourite Bible characters. He was a gifted, favoured and ambitious teenager who made some outrageous claims about his future – as many teenagers have done throughout time. The effect of his claims was probably rather more dramatic than he anticipated, however. He found himself brutally mistreated, sold into slavery, bought by a fine household, falsely accused and dumped in a dungeon before his dreams were realised.

The process to which he was subjected took thirteen weary years before it was complete. On numerous occasions he must have felt that his dreams were no more than a great illusion. He had many opportunities to become bitter, but instead he allowed the circumstances he faced to shape his character for the better. Although he was unable to choose where he lived during those thirteen years, he carefully chose his reactions to the events that unfolded. The Bible records repeatedly that 'The Lord was with him' (Genesis 39:2, 3, 21, 23). Not in the ease of a fulfilled dream, but in the discipline of frustrated desire. He chose to behave correctly, believing wholeheartedly what God had shown him in his teenage dream, and eventually his ambitions were fulfilled. Because he had trusted God and triumphed in the years of adversity, all he needed was a shave and a change of clothes to fit him for his future as ruler of Egypt, second only to Pharaoh himself. Joseph's home moved from prison to palace overnight. In this long experience he learned that the very worst his enemies could do to him was sell him into the promise and purpose of God.

The Bible says of Joseph's life:

> 'Until the time that his word came, the word of Lord tried him.'   (Psalm 105:19, KJV)

I have never forgotten these words since reading them as a boy of sixteen, seeking to live out the same principles that

Joseph exercised with an unwavering confidence that whatever God has promised He will accomplish. Adherence to the principles so clearly stated in Bible truth, when obeyed, will not fail to align my life with God's purpose. He uses every vicissitude, like the refiner's heat, to produce the pure metal of a prepared life, readying me to enjoy my promised land.

A wise gardener once presented his granddaughter with an apple tree, instructing her to plant it with bricks beneath to hinder formation of the tap root, thus constraining the tree to send roots sideways for greater stability and fruitfulness. The purpose of adverse circumstances is not to hold us **back** but to hold us **in**, preparing us for greater fruitfulness. So even in adversity, now is the time, not for bluster and self-promotion, nor for passive acceptance, but for active, daily choices of living right, not blaming but trusting God, not moaning but maintaining faith and not succumbing but overcoming the negative situations around you. The need for and appreciation of an active and decisive approach to life must be tempered with the positive mind of confidence in God, which is worked in us through right responses to adversity and testing.

Joseph clearly maintained his priorities after his transition from prison to palace, successfully developing a difficult economy and the various relational levels of his remarkable life. This is particularly impressive when one considers how many of us allow the urgent things of other people's lives to dominate the use of our time. How can we guard against such intrusions? First, we must have a clear view of what is important. What am I aiming for? What is my goal? What has God said? Answer these questions and our purpose will come more sharply into focus, enabling us to re-prioritise what is important.

Such concepts have been ably addressed by a number of time management gurus, most notably Stephen Covey. He shows the balance between **importance** and **urgency** as illustrated in Figure 1.

The contents of the four quadrants may be summarised **action**, **quality**, **deception** and **waste**, or more informally,

	Urgent	**Not urgent**
Important	**I** ● Crises ● Pressing problems ● Deadline-driven projects, meetings, preparations	**II** ● Preparation ● Prevention ● Values clarification ● Planning ● Relationship building ● True re-creation ● Empowerment
Not important	**III** ● Interruptions, some phone calls ● Some mail, some reports ● Some meetings ● Many proximate, pressing matters ● Many popular activities	**IV** ● Trivia, busywork ● Junk mail ● Some phone calls ● Time wasters ● 'Escape' activities

Figure 1

do it, schedule it, delegate it and **forget it**. The key to success in the battle between the urgent and important for our lives is to move from the **not-important-but-urgent** things (Quadrant 3) into the better-planned use of time focusing on **important-but-not-urgent** activity (Quadrant 2). Covey illustrates this by comparing high performance organisations with typical ones. The significant difference between the two is in their apportioning of time to Quadrants 2 and 3 (see Figure 2).

Covey says:

'The degree to which urgency drives the organisation is the degree to which importance does not. This is not to suggest that there is no urgency. Quadrant 1 is very real and a good percentage of time should be spent doing

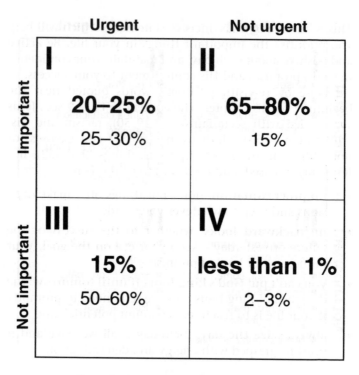

Figure 2 (percentages in bold type represent
high-performance organizations)

things that are both urgent and important. But so
much time is wasted in Quadrant 3, because importance isn't clear!'

What is important to us in the pilgrimage of life? We may
be in a state of survival and dependency, but is our direction
'across the river', through the final obstacles before those
we will encounter in our promised land? Is the correct use
of your time a giant against which you struggle? Does it
block your progress? It is both urgent and important to
know what is of greatest importance in your life, so spend
some time clarifying this issue. If you're a Christian,

> *'Seek first the Kingdom of God and His righteousness, and
> all these things will be added to you.'*   (Matthew 6:33)

This is but one of Jesus' incisive statements which will help you prioritise the important things in your life. Be active and positive about each day, and maintain your confidence in God's promises and His commitment to your success.

I close by re-visiting Christ's words quoted near the beginning of this chapter. The context in Luke 9 sees Jesus surrounded with sectarianism (9:49, 50), racism and discrimination (9:53), vindictiveness (9:54) and excuses for not addressing the most important things (9:57–62). But Jesus stays focused, and invites us to be the same:

- **no procrastination**: don't put things off – make decisions and keep to whatever you decide;

- **no backward looks**: whether to the success or the failure of yesterday – keep your eye on the goal, your purpose, your land of promise;

- **you can't put God's kingdom off until tomorrow**: the demands of King Jesus must be responded to promptly if your life is to reach its maximum potential; and

- always **seize the day**, for today is all we have and it must be grasped with energy and determination.

Chapter 6

Your Mind is Your Business

> If everybody minded their business, the world would go round a great deal faster than it does.

One's mind is very much one's own business, but many people live in ignorant irresponsibility towards their own minds. The Apostle Paul offers an exciting alternative.

> *'The mind controlled by the Spirit is life and peace.'*
>
> (Romans 8:6)

He goes on to say how our minds can be transformed and renewed, giving us the ability to know God's best for our lives. The Bible is very honest in pointing out the dark side of man's nature when left without God's help. We should look with care at what it teaches; it could make the difference as to whether we live successfully or otherwise.

Let us consider the dark side of the subject first. The awful truth should make us serious about leaving it behind. Paul clearly recognised the mind for the battleground it is.

> *'Once you were alienated from God and were enemies in your minds because of your evil behaviour.'*
>
> (Colossians 1:21)

He further said that we all lived at one time *'gratifying the cravings of our sinful nature and following its desires and thoughts'* (Ephesians 2:3). To another group of early Christians he wrote,

> *'The god of this age has blinded the minds of unbelievers, so that they cannot see the light of the gospel.'*
> (2 Corinthians 4:4)

Then in a blistering attack he insisted that Christians should,

> *'No longer live as the Gentiles do in the futility of their thinking, [since] they are darkened in their understanding and separated from the life of God because of the ignorance that is in them due to the hardening of their hearts. Having lost all sensitivity, they have given themselves over to sensuality so as to indulge in every kind of impurity, with a continual lust for more.'* (Ephesians 4:17–19)

Not very nice! In summary, without God's help we become educated fools with upset minds and sick bodies; bitter-hearted people struggling with uncontrolled lust, whose minds are so blinded to reality we don't even think we have a problem. If you doubt the reality and accuracy of this description of the human race, pick up a copy of today's newspaper and consider the recorded events. But there is some good news also: following the passage quoted above, Paul continues,

> *'You, however, did not come to know Christ that way ... You were taught, with regard to your former way of life, to put off your old self, which is being corrupted by its deceitful desires; to be made new in the attitude of your minds; and to put on the new self, created to be like God in true righteousness and holiness.'* (Ephesians 4:20–24)

Furthermore, this new mind *'will be able to test and approve what God's will is'* (Romans 12:2). It will have the ability to overcome anxiety (Philippians 4:6), and God also promises to put a new set of laws in our minds (Hebrews 8:10; 10:15), while encouraging us to *'prepare [our] minds for action'* (1 Peter 1:13). We must learn to put a new guard around our minds; God wants His peace to guard our hearts. When

your peace of heart and mind goes, that is a warning that
enemy troops – wrong thoughts – are in the area.

Before proceeding to the truth of how our minds are
renewed, a few questions must be asked. What do you think
about God? Until you see God on His throne and in control,
you will not be confident about the future. What do you
think about the Church? Until you see the Church as *'the
fullness of Him who fills everything in every way'* (Ephesians
1:23) your future will have limited fulfilment. What do you
think about the devil? Until you see him crushed under
your feet by the power of the God of peace (Romans 16:20),
you will have limited victory. And finally, what do you
think about yourself? Judge neither by what other people
have said, nor by what you have thought. Only by changing
your thinking to agree with what God thinks about you will
you have a future full of victory and potential.

1. So how do we renew our mind?

The Bible says that you should

> *'Be transformed by the renewing of your mind.'*
>
> (Romans 12:2)

'Transformed' means 'the obligation to undergo a complete
change which under the power of God will find expression
in character and conduct,' and is translated from the Greek
metamorphoo. From this we take the English word 'meta-
morphosis' – the caterpillar forming a chrysalis and
changing into a butterfly. God wants us to co-operate with
His power and ability so that our minds are changed into
something entirely different, and made new again. By
repentance and accepting God's salvation, the power is
made available to us – but we must then co-operate with
right action. Back to Ephesians 4 again:

> *'Each of you must put off falsehood and speak truthfully ...
> "In your anger do not sin": Do not let the sun go down while
> you are still angry, and do not give the devil a foothold. He
> who has been stealing must steal no longer, but must work*

> *... **do not** let any unwholesome talk come out of your mouths, but only what is helpful for building others up ... Do not grieve the Holy Spirit of God ... Get rid of all bitterness, rage and anger, brawling and slander, along with every kind of malice.'*   (Ephesians 4:25–31)

Lest these should seem rather negative commands, Paul gives us a positive alternative:

> *'Be kind and compassionate to one another, forgiving each other ... Be imitators of God ... Live a life of love.'*
> (Ephesians 4:32–5:2)

Self-control of our words, thoughts, emotions and actions is therefore the secret to the renewed mind-life we are seeking.

This is all very well as a neat little Bible study, but it must be worked out in our lives through diligent action, regardless of how we feel. 'Oh, I've fallen out with my wife, but she was in the wrong; let her apologise first.' 'I don't feel very well; I don't think I shall bother going to work today.' You can imagine many other situations where wrong feelings bring about a wrong confession and result in idleness. We will never keep our minds renewed with behaviour like that. Self-control must be exercised not only to avoid the pitfalls of sin in life's journey, but also to spur us into positive action.

2. Take every thought captive

We must take every thought captive, because what we think controls the way we live. Before any word has crossed our lips, before any act is worked out through our body, a thought has crossed our mind. Consider this wisdom:

> *'There are six things the Lord hates, seven that are detestable to Him: haughty eyes, a lying tongue, hands that shed innocent blood, a heart that devises wicked schemes, feet that are quick to rush into evil, a false witness who pours out lies and a man who stirs up dissension among brothers.'*
> (Proverbs 6:16–19)

'He who guards his lips guards his life, but he who speaks rashly will come to ruin.' (Proverbs 13:3)

'Do not let your heart envy sinners, but always be zealous for the fear of the Lord. There is surely a future hope for you, and your hope will not be cut off.' (Proverbs 23:17)

The requirement implicit in these proverbs is the capture and exchange of any wrong thought, and they hint at the development of thoughts into words and actions. But how do you capture your thoughts? You have a pain and think, 'I must be ill! I'm going to die!' Someone is delayed on their way home, and you become anxious. 'Have they had an accident?' Faced with a new challenge, you might think and say, 'I don't think I can do it.' These are the sort of thoughts which must be captured. The Greek word *aichmalotizo*, translated 'captive', carries the literal sense of 'taken by the spear', implying that thoughts are to be caught, controlled, pinned to the ground and changed.

Many people are so used to wrong thinking and speaking that they have developed 'rabbit trails' in their thought life – automatic responses, negative thoughts of fear and failure. We must change our thought patterns, capturing them a thousand times if necessary, and exchange them for right thinking: the thinking of God and the words of the Bible. The way to change is to learn the thoughts of God (Jeremiah 29:11; Psalm 40:17), meditate on His words (Joshua 1:8), and walk with people who live by these principles (Proverbs 13:20). The Psalmist prayed, *'Try me and know my thoughts'* (Psalm 139:23). Ask God, 'Help me to think as you want me to think.' You'll be amazed at how different your life will become.

3. Control that tongue

The Duke of Wellington was once asked, 'If you had your life over again, what would you change?' 'I'd give more praise,' he answered. The tongue may be used very power-fully to positive or negative effect. Among many comments, the Bible says that:

> *'The tongue has the power of life and death, and those who love it will eat its fruit.'*   (Proverbs 18:21)

Also,

> *'Whoever of you loves life and desires to see many good days, keep your tongue from evil and your lips from speaking lies.'*   (Psalm 34:12, 13)

So many people are careless with their speech. A harsh word to a young child can cause horrendous damage. Tired and frustrated, a misplaced word from a teacher can harm a student. Unkind words rooted in bad feeling can finish a marriage. There is no doubt that words are powerful:

> *'Reckless words pierce like a sword.'*   (Proverbs 12:18)

The reverse is equally true: words of love and encouragement will benefit a child and enhance a marriage; gentle correction and direction will strengthen the student. Words of comfort, encouragement and strength are the hallmarks of prophecy in 1 Corinthians 14. Do not therefore curse yourself or others by careless speech. Every day you may hear people say, 'I must be out of my mind,' or in speaking to a child, 'You stupid boy!' Making sure that the business of our mind is in proper order, each of us must put a guard over our mouth against negative speaking. Note James' warning and get the hell out of your mouth:

> *'The tongue ... is a fire, a world of evil among all the parts of the body. It corrupts the whole person, sets the whole course of his life on fire, and is itself set on fire by hell.'*
> (James 3:6)

Strong words, but excellence must be aimed at; the benefits are invaluable:

> *'If anyone is never at fault in what he says, he is a perfect man, able to keep his whole body in check.'*   (James 3:2)

As you are able, use your tongue in speaking a prayer with me:

'Lord Jesus, please help me to renew my mind, help me to think as you want me to think. Teach me how to take every thought captive and in controlling my tongue, bring glory to you. Amen.'

4. Anoint my head

We all need the help of God's Spirit anointing and affecting our thinking. Wisdom comes from God and is of greater value than understanding and knowledge, though each have their important place. When our forefather Adam lost his innocence and fell with Eve into deception, part of the allure offered to them was to *'gain wisdom'* (Genesis 3:6). The New Testament counsels us:

> *'If any of you lacks wisdom, he should ask God, who gives generously to all without finding fault, and it will be given to him.'*
> (James 1:5)

Adam and Eve made three critical mistakes, and we would do well to learn from them:

- they listened to the wrong advice and were therefore **deceived** (Genesis 3:1–5);
- they looked at the wrong values and were therefore **disobedient** (Genesis 3:6–7);
- they lied about their wrongdoing and began to live in **denial** (Genesis 3:12).

The dreadful long-term consequences of their behaviour should cause us to think. If they had listened to God and accepted His value system, how different things could have been! Outside of salvation, the human race continues to be deceived, lives in disobedience and issues a constant denial of responsibility. Remember Adam's response to God:

> *'The woman **you** put here with me, **she** gave me . . . '*
> (Genesis 3:12)

Pathetic, isn't it? But rest assured we're no better! All around us people are making excuses, shifting the blame, and living in denial of their sinful condition. A change of heart is necessary here. David spoke gratefully of God's disciplinary intervention in his life:

'Let the Righteous One strike me – it is a kindness; let Him rebuke me – it is oil on my head. My head will not refuse it.'
(Psalm 141:5)

Speaking prophetically of Jesus Christ, Isaiah wrote:

'The Spirit of the Lord will rest on Him – the Spirit of wisdom and of understanding, the Spirit of counsel and of power, the Spirit of knowledge and of the fear of the Lord – and He will delight in the fear of the Lord.'
(Isaiah 11:2, 3)

God's Spirit can give us natural and spiritual insight, wisdom and knowledge in order that the business of our minds is properly conducted. Two simple illustrations come to my mind. My manager once asked me for some figures, knowing that all our current procedures would not easily produce them. 'I must have hard data to give to the divisional manager. Find a way to get it, David!' After some time working (and praying) at my desk, an inspiration came that gave me an entirely different method for obtaining the required information. It was quicker and more accurate than the technique we'd used previously, and the boss was pleased. I believe that God 'anointed my head' with the wisdom I needed.

When my son Jonathan was much younger, he once asked me 'Dad, why can't I call you David like everyone else?' An entirely spontaneous reply came from my mouth: 'There is no reason Jonathan, except that you are the only little boy in the world who can call me Daddy.' I never heard any more on the subject. Jonathan is now a 'family man' in his own right, and our relationship is very different, but he still calls me Dad and I am pleased about that.

I have deliberately used simple illustrations here to make the possibilities more attainable. Dramatic examples can make the experience seem unreachable. God will anoint your head, sometimes surprising you!

In conclusion, my mind is my business and your mind is your business. I have known these truths for some years now, maybe like you, but writing them today reinforces my confidence in them, and my determination to practise what I preach. Each one of us, for successful promised land living, must renew our mindset, capture and exchange wrong thinking, keep control of our tongue and live with the help of God's Spirit. Our minds will then be positive and fruitful. Remember, your mind is your business, so mind your own business!

Chapter 7

Thinking Big and Seeing Clearly

'When I grow up, I'm going to drive a fire engine.' For a four-year-old boy, that is a grand ambition. Every generation the world over knows about this 'one-day' dream. Similarly, many people hold an ambition for economic migration: witness the brown line in Texas, and movement into western Europe from Africa or the old Eastern bloc. In times past, people have emigrated *en masse* to North America, New Zealand and Australia – all in search of a better life. And thousands keep making such journeys, for this 'better life' search is to be found in every human heart. The grass is always greener on the other side. But just as 'one-day' ambitions are insufficient by themselves, 'better-life' aspirations rarely deliver their promise. The world needs people who have seen what is un-seeable and grasped the impossible – people who think big and see clearly.

During the reconnaissance of Canaan described in Numbers 13, Joshua and Caleb saw more than a 'better life'. They saw more than the geographical reality of the Prom-ised Land. What do I mean? The ten other leaders standing with Joshua and Caleb saw only the physical circumstances. They saw it, but they didn't see it! In their report, these others said, *'the land we explored devours those living in it'* (Numbers 13:32). However, in the face of the despair and hostility generated by this claim, Joshua and Caleb told everybody:

*'The land we passed through and explored is exceedingly
good. If the Lord is pleased with us, He will lead us into the
land, a land flowing with milk and honey, and will give it to
us. Only do not rebel against the Lord. And do not be afraid
of the people of the land, because we will swallow them up.
Their protection is gone, but the Lord is with us. Do not be
afraid of them.'*   (Numbers 14:7–9)

The consequence of their farsightedness was profound:
among their peers, companions and contemporaries,
Joshua and Caleb alone were to eventually live in and enjoy
that which they had seen with their natural eyes.

The world needs people with this sort of vision. But
before we seek to develop it, how may we define it? My
dictionary says that 'vision' is 'the ability of, or an aptitude
for, great perception or foresight, especially relating to
future developments.' Jonathan Swift said, 'Vision is the
art of seeing things invisible.' Winston Churchill held that
'The great thing is to get the true picture, whatever it is.'
Costa Diaz claimed that 'If you cannot see the invisible, you
will never enjoy the impossible.' The working definition we
shall use is coloured by these statements. To have vision is
to see in one's heart what cannot be physically seen. In
part, this is by natural perception, but it also comes by
revelation. From a strictly Christian viewpoint, if we believe
that God sees and knows everything and has a desire to
share His plans with us, we must make ourselves available
to receive revelation from Him. How does this work out in
practice?

Vision and imagination

The dimension of our personality we call imagination is
part of our humanity, given to us by God. In the book of
Acts, Peter repeats Joel's prophecy to an attentive crowd:

*'In the last days, God says, "I will pour out my Spirit on all
people. Your sons daughters will prophesy, your young men
will see visions, your old men will dream dreams." '*

(Acts 2:17)

Some Christians have cried 'Occult!' at the very suggestion that the right use of imagination and visualisation might have a valuable part to play in the realm of dreams and visions. Of course there is danger: every good and godly thing is counterfeited. Yet the most effective measure against deception is not obsession with the imitation, but to constantly handle the real thing. Bank tellers swiftly learn to recognise fraudulent notes by constantly handling authentic ones.

David Yonggi Cho, whose work for God in Korea is one of the outstanding Christian testimonies of the 20th century, has been criticised by well-meaning but ill-informed Christians, whose personal experience of the areas in question lack the mature level of understanding brought about by usage. For myself, I have frequently 'imagined' things that later proved to be accurate information, useful for prophecy, words of knowledge and other encouraging gifts of the Spirit. While remaining aware of the wrong use of imagination and visualisation (as championed by the New Age movement, and used historically within Buddhism) we should not allow this misuse to detract from the right use of these faculties. Rather, we should practise every godly exercise, including the correct use of our imagination, for the glory of Jesus Christ and the benefit of His creation.

Vision and prophecy

> *'Saul's servant said "Look in this town there is a man of God, he is highly respected, and everything he says comes true. Let's go there now. Perhaps he will tell us what way to take."'* (1 Samuel 9:6)

There is tremendous power in prophecy. While not confusing the prophetic word with Scripture, we must not mistake prophecy to be merely human words. Somehow God's breath is in them, and when repeated, they live again. I was recently in Lerwick on the wind-swept but beautiful Shetland Islands. In one meeting I spoke at, someone reminded the congregation of a prophecy given twenty years previously:

> 'When men say, "It is impossible," I, the Lord, will do it.'

Even writing the words releases new life in me! It seems to me that one of the tests of the strength of prophecy is its ability, when repeated, to live again and inspire afresh.

What about the interface between vision and prophecy? The great prophets of the Bible knew far more about prophetic power than I have just expressed. They spoke of what they saw, whether it was obvious and visible, or invisible and perceived solely by themselves. Whether it was the secret wisdom of God, advice in a difficult situation or action to fulfil the will of God, they spoke whatever they saw in prophecy to truly dramatic effect. Amos, one of the minor prophets whose prophecies have such powerful contemporary significance, explained that:

> *'The Sovereign Lord does nothing without revealing His plan to His servants the prophets.'*
> (Amos 3:7)

Sometimes a dream, sometimes a vision, sometimes a parable or a prophetic action, the lengths God goes to in order to communicate with His people are impressive. And all because He wants them to see the way He wishes them to take.

Jonah was instructed by God to go to Nineveh, but was reluctant to go. He did not want God to forgive the wicked Ninevites, yet he knew He would. After his excursion in the big fish, the Bible records his message from God. Only eight words, but potent enough to change the heart of a city:

> *'Forty more days and Nineveh will be overturned.'*
> (Jonah 3:4)

The most powerful, despotic empire in the world at the time crumbled in repentance as a consequence. What about the post-exilic prophets Haggai and Zechariah? Together they confronted a discouraged, disillusioned, unsuccessful people, none of whom were enjoying their promised land.

However, they were inspired into performing meaningful and productive work, their lives redirected and energised by the two seers who spoke the word of God. Much more could be said about the rest of the biblical prophets, visionaries and seers, who by speaking what God showed them transformed countless situations.

What of today? Is it realistic to believe that people can see the un-seeable, and speak the prophetic word with power? Everything in me says 'Yes!' and longs to play a part. God always works to a purpose and a plan, and always, according to Amos, reveals His plan to His people through His prophets. The presence of a prophetic edge of vision and foresight in our lives will increase our ability to take our promised land.

Vision and potential

Insight (truly seeing what already exists) and foresight (discerning the future) are both important components of vision. As such, they are vital to the effective release of your potential. Unless you know where you are aiming to go or what you are aiming to do, how can you measure your success? Martin Luther King had a dream: he saw the potential for black America to be set free from the oppression under which they laboured, and it gave direction to his life.

Jesus spent His life giving direction and purpose to people, releasing the potential that He saw in them despite the circumstances surrounding them. To some fishermen He said,

> '*Come, follow me ... and I will make you fishers of men.*'
> (Matthew 4:19)

While looking over a city whose people needed change, He said,

> '*Do you not say, "Four months more and then the harvest"? I tell you, open your eyes and look at the fields! They are ripe for harvest.*'   (John 4:35)

Hearing that his friend Lazarus was sick, He saw the opportunity for God to receive greater glory through Lazarus' death and resurrection (John 11:1–44). Most people saw Zacchaeus as a short, cheating taxman, but Jesus saw someone else: Jesus saw the potential in Zacchaeus, so He called him out of the tree and invited Himself to dinner (Luke 19:1–10).

I could go on and on. Throughout the Gospels, we read how Jesus released either people or situations to their full potential because He had sufficient vision to see the possibilities dormant within them. One of the great joys of life is to realise the potential in people and see them develop the gifts God has put within them. We need the help of God to see existing, visible or hidden possibilities in our life and the lives of those around us. This path requires faith, daring and endurance, but it offers great rewards.

Vision and progress

If we have seen something, we can work toward it and stay inspired until we hold and enjoy that which we envisaged. The life of any community – be it a family, company, church or a whole country – will benefit greatly if the vision is clearly stated, firmly believed and corporately expressed by all involved. Bryn Hughes once showed me the diagram in Figure 3. It helped me understand the relationship between vision and progress in the life of a community of people. Its two axes represent the degree to which vision is clear and common. When vision is clear but diverse, **division** results; when vision is diverse and vague, the community suffers **attrition**; common but vague vision generates **frustration**. Only when the vision is both clear and common, seen and shared by all, can the community enjoy **cohesion** and togetherness.

I have observed the truth of this principle directly in many churches, but its application is far broader. So many groups fail to progress as they should because they lack clarity of vision and are careless in reaching agreement amongst themselves about what their vision truly is.

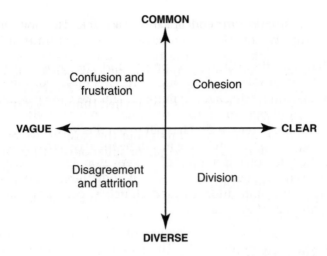

Figure 3 *Unity in vision*

Vision and motivation

Nehemiah was a man of passion and vision. He strongly desired to see Jerusalem rebuilt. In the face of intimidation, compromise and time wasting, his vision drove him forward and motivated his life. He and his companions believed that 'the task ahead of them was nothing compared to the power behind them.'[1]

History is full of people who saw something invisible, who were motivated and energised to discover, adventure, travel, and accomplish feats of daring beyond normal expectation. The Church of Jesus needs this motivation; it therefore needs vision. Western democracies need new energy and motivation to overcome the huge social and moral catastrophe that threatens to engulf them.

> *'Where there is no revelation* [Hebrew *hazon* – vision], *the people cast off restraint.'* (Proverbs 29:18)

Where there is no clear boundary, the people lack motivation and live negligent lives. In the book of Samuel we read:

[1] Attributed to Dave Cave.

'In those days the word of the Lord was rare; there were not many visions.'   (1 Samuel 3:1)

What was the result? The priests and the people lived carelessly, displeased God, and were soon enslaved, suffering loss and serving a mean purpose. This has close parallels in much of our world. Each of us needs our own vision, a sight of the potential God has put in our life. When we have seen it, we immediately live in a different way. What is true for the individual is also true for every grouping in society. We need prophets who have seen something, who give clarity and motivation to tired churches, companies and countries as they speak.

Vision and you

Are you content with the 'fire engine' vision I started with, the attitude that 'maybe one day I'll be something'? I hope not. Most people – Christian or not – aspire no higher than the 'better-life' vision: 'I want two cars, three children, four bedrooms, five friends and a six-figure salary. Then I'll be all right.' But we were all created for more than this. We need to see the invisible!

We must first see the greatness of the invisible God. In Him and His plans we see the possibilities of our life. These possibilities are unrealised potential. Each of us has an opportunity to realise our potential. The major emphasis of each life differs. Some excel in service and give their actions; others as thinkers give their minds. Still others as providers give their resources. The list is wide and varied. The genius of the Creator and creation is that everyone has a part and all can be fulfilled. I am sure His plan is bigger than we think and His desire is that we see it more clearly than we have previously seen. Erasmus said 'In the country of the blind, the one-eyed man is king.' In a more contemporary sense, 'Information is power.' Vision is comprised of insight, revelation, intuition, direction, and information – and carries power with it. God wants us to enjoy an adventure, opening our eyes, helping us to see what others cannot see.

The author P.D. James expressed the mediocrity of vision-less life saying:

> 'We need, all of us, to be in control of our lives, and we shrink them until they're small and mean enough so that we can feel in control.'

This position is far from God's ideal. Lack of vision and the rarity of the Word of the Lord have had the same effect upon us as they did on the people in Samuel's time, mentioned above. We need the heart to say to God, *'Speak, for your servant is listening'* (1 Samuel 3:10), and the humility to pray 'Lord, anoint my eyes that I may see.' In this hearing and seeing, thinking big and seeing clearly come within our reach. The resultant clarity opens the way to success – living in our promised land of fulfilled potential.

Chapter 8

Welcome Three Old Friends – Faith, Hope and Love

Our journey into the promised land is progressing. If we look over our shoulder it should only be to remind ourselves that now is the time, today is the day of opportunity. We changed and are still changing our minds, renewing them, a very necessary step for living in this new place. Opening our minds has helped us to open our eyes. We may be daunted by the bigger, clearer picture, but we are pressing forward. We know, whatever the challenges, where we were born to live. How do we maintain our focus, keep up our energy levels and stay motivated? We need these three old friends, Faith, Hope and Love. They have been working their magic since the dawn of time. The early chapters of the Bible reveal Abraham as a man of great faith – he believed God – a good thing to do! Noah had hope for the future salvation of his family when by faith he built the ark. Lot saw the whole plain of Jordan was well watered (Genesis 13:10), and had hope for a prosperous future. Imagine working fourteen years, to marry the woman you love as Jacob did for Rachel (Genesis 29). In every culture, in every time, faith, hope and love have played their part in successful living.

The Bible says in the passage so often read at weddings:

> 'Now these three remain: faith, hope and love. But the greatest of these is love.' (1 Corinthians 13:13)

The book of Hebrews links faith and hope together, declaring:

> *'Now faith is being sure of what we hope for...'*
>
> (Hebrews 11:1)

Hope is a favorable and confident expectation – and has to do with the unseen and the future. Faith is a conviction based on hearing. When our expectation becomes reality and our conviction in what cannot be seen becomes visible, then faith and hope have done their work. They are soon off to find another project. Love however, is always needed – it never fails.

Much has been written about these three friends and for very good reasons. Imagine life without hope. It would indeed be 'hopeless' for *'hope is an anchor for the soul'* (Hebrews 6:19). Likewise, life without faith cannot please God (Hebrews 11:6) and life without love is a cold and miserable journey.

I recently read a quotation from Alexander Chambers which said:

> 'The three grand essentials of happiness are: Something to do, Someone to love and Something to hope for.'

As the book of Psalms often recommends, *selah* – think about that.

- To *do* something requires **conviction** – a word associated with faith.

- To *love* brings a release of passion often linked with inspiration.

- To *hope* requires expectation and helps us look forward and continue our pilgrimage.

Chambers is expressing the work of our three friends as essential for happiness. I shared these ideas with a group of leaders recently and found myself expressing the concepts in a slightly different way. I speak of love first because it never fails and will be with us into eternity. God is love. Love is pre-eminent. Someone to love, quoting Chambers again, provides the motivation, the driving force for our lives. I am not speaking about the self-seeking, pleasure-hungry portrayal of love on celluloid from Hollywood. I mean the self-sacrificing *agape* of God which He longs to distribute into each of our lives. This love, received only from God and reciprocated by the wise, blesses all the other legitimate loves of our life. Furthermore, all the passion, inspiration and motivation needed to live successful lives flows out of receiving this love. If motivation comes when we have someone to love, then purpose gives us something to do. The opposite of this is action without design or rational, where life drifts by and there is no reason or plan to our existence – a dangerous and very unfulfilling way to live. Did someone say 'The devil finds work for idle hands'? When we understand that God designed us for a reason, provided us with all the needed ingredients to fulfil His purpose, and opened the door into our promised land through the Lord Jesus, our days of aimless drifting will be over for ever. By the way, as a bonus, you will be charged with energy as you pursue God's purpose for you – a great feeling.

It is important that we direct this energy. We need a destination, somewhere to go. We can discover our destiny when we focus on our destination. The modern use of the word destiny has connotations of fate – what will be, will be. This idea leaves us in a reactive position, and that is not part of promised land living. Reactive thinking brings back the specter of victim thinking and can leave us paralyzed. We may not be able to change our circumstances but, promised land thinking changes our approach to our circumstances. We believe that God has a plan for our lives, but without our active co-operation and involvement it will not materialize, because He will not force His will upon us.

God spoke to me many times when I was a young man. I am extremely grateful for those encounters. Believing and processing that which I understood God to have said helped bring into focus both the destiny and destination of my life. It has required diligent work; the giants must be killed. I have sometimes lost my focus, been distracted, or believed a lie. This promised land adventure is not an afternoon picnic by a babbling stream, although the pilgrimage has many such happy moments along the pathway. It is a journey of occupation. Breaking all the chains in our minds and lives and possessing what God has promised is an exciting but blood-stained journey!

With the motivation gained from having **someone to love**, we understand something of our purpose giving us **something to do** and our destiny shows us **somewhere to go**. Our friend Hope points forward offering aspiration and expectation. The dictionary meaning of aspiration is 'drawing of breath; desire; action'. The Christian has a wonderful advantage in the hope stakes, for God is a God of hope (Romans 15:13). He is the author of it, not its subject. It comes from Him. All men need hope. I have already said that, without hope, life is hopeless, depression is just around the corner, despair is not much further distant, and may terminate in suicide; a horrible bunch of terrors we can live without. But the Bible promises us a living hope (1 Peter 1:3) and a blessed hope (Titus 2:13).

> *'Praise be to God the Father of our Lord Jesus Christ! In His great mercy He has given us new birth into a living hope through the resurrection of Jesus Christ from the dead and into an inheritance that can never perish, spoil or fade.'*
>
> (1 Peter 1:3)

Jesus has conquered man's greatest enemy – death – and offers each person His help in all the good and bad experiences of life – Whoopee! Have you actively taken hold of the gift of new birth into a living hope? What a spring that puts into your step!

Some people ask, 'Why are you so committed to Jesus? Surely there have been many great teachers in history.' Indeed there have. Like Jesus they were all born into this world, they lived distinguished lives in their unique way and then they all died – including Jesus Christ. But only Jesus claimed a power beyond death: *'I am the resurrection and the life,'* He said, (John 11:25) because only Jesus conquered death in what we call the resurrection. His unique 'livingness' (a well attested historic fact) and His continuing impact in the world (an unquestionable truth) are both part of the reason why I am so committed to Jesus. As my dear friend, evangelist J. John says,

> 'If you met two men at a crossroads, one living and one dead – which one would you take directions from?'

Jesus' power over death gives me hope. I have a future expectation. With His living help I can face all that life puts in my pathway. Another friend recently passed an anonymous quote to me:

> 'Confucius said "I know the way." Krishna said, "I see the way." Mohammed said, "I am a prophet of the way." Buddha said, "I am seeking the way." The New Age Movement says, "We are on the way." Only Jesus said, "**I am the way.**" '

What a hope!

Beyond this living hope we can enjoy what the Bible calls a blessed hope.

> '... we wait for the blessed hope – the glorious appearing of our great God and Saviour, Jesus Christ.'   (Titus 2:13)

The early Christians lived with urgency. They were looking for the return of Jesus. The young church at Thessalonica was a classic example. As shown in Paul's first letter they are waiting and expectant (1 Thessalonians 1:10). The next chapter finds Paul inspired by them (2:19). They are encouraged to live blameless and holy lives (3:13). Then Paul instructs them further about the events surrounding the physical return of Jesus Christ (4:13–18) telling them to 'encourage each other with these words' (4:18). The book ends with a mass of practical advice, calling them to be 'blameless at the coming of our Lord Jesus Christ' (5:23).

I grew up in an environment where the return of Jesus was strongly preached. Many argued passionately about when and how this would occur. Some of the teaching had an escapist mentality: 'Don't be involved in the affairs of this present world, because we are leaving. Heaven is our

home.' This approach meant the 'salt' of their witness and
the impact of their 'light' upon the darkness was less than it
could have been. Today the pendulum of teaching seems to
have swung too far in the opposite direction. The Western
church needs to hear the demanding message that Jesus is
coming again! It is a blessed hope.

My wife Dorothy Ann brought home an old picture of her
Grandma today. The picture carries a story. Given to her
teenage sweetheart with a simple message of affection, the
picture was returned to her after he was killed in active
service during the First World War. Even in such sad
circumstances, all who have truly trusted Jesus Christ for
forgiveness and salvation have a hope. One day we will
meet those who have already entered the presence of God.
All sadness, pain and sorrow will be ended. While we live,
we watch with expectation, living our lives to please God
and working to see God's kingdom extended on earth.
When we die or when Christ returns, we will say 'to be
with Christ ... is better by far!' (Philippians 1:23). We look
forward to a blessed hope both in life and beyond the grave.

'*And now these three remain: Faith, Hope and Love*'
(1 Corinthians 13:13). We need them every day for motivation, purpose, destiny and aspiration. They will prove good
companions. They travel well on the roads both towards
and within our promised land. E. Stanley Jones said:

'When life kicks you; let it kick you forward.'

I suggest our three trusted friends will help that to happen if
we let them.

Chapter 9

Coming to Rest

Holding on to hope in the face of a given challenge is commendable, but the typical human response in awkward situations is to hold on to anxiety instead. For some years now, the medical establishment has been warning us of the detrimental effects of anxiety and stress on the human body. In extreme cases, stress is a killer. Is the solution to do nothing? Should we persevere against opposition, or give in when confronted with adversity? A workaholic is as dangerous as any other addict, yet the wisdom of the ages tells us that:

> *'All hard work brings a profit, but mere talk leads only to poverty.'*   (Proverbs 14:23)

How can we find a sensible balance between work and rest, stress and relief, pressure and pleasure? Life cannot be composed of swinging from one extreme to the other. We cannot all opt out of life's rush for an easy existence on a quiet island or some country estate, so how and where are we to find the elusive secret of rest within our work? Jesus Christ said,

> *'Are you tired? ... Come to me, get away with me and you'll recover your life. I'll show you how to take a real rest. Walk with me and work with me, watch how I do it. Learn the unforced rhythms of grace. I won't lay anything heavy or ill-fitting on you. Keep company with me and you'll learn to live freely and lightly.'*   (Matthew 11:28–30, *The Message*)

This is surely the goal at which we're aiming. I don't think Jesus means us to schedule regular visits away for a contemplative retreat, although such practices are a useful pit-stop in the race of our lives. He offers to teach us a much more dynamic way of living, working and resting. In the New Testament, the Greek word *katapausis*, frequently translated as 'rest', can be understood to mean 'to cause to cease, to restrain; an active resting'. What can that phrase mean? Vine defines the related word *anapausis* (which is also translated 'rest') thus:

> 'Christ's rest is not rest from work, but rest in work. Not the rest of inactivity but of the harmonious working of all the faculties and affections – of will, heart, imagination, conscience – because each has found in God the ideal sphere for its satisfaction and development.'

That sounds highly desirable: not rest **from** work, but rest **in** work, as every part of my personality lives in orchestrated harmony. The very idea is both relaxing, peaceful and exhilarating. This is the rest into which Christ offers to lead us – a rest very different from the human's exhausted collapse when tired out and over-stressed.

How do we reach this place of active rest? Before good feelings of well-being overtake us as we stand here in sight of our goal, let us face some facts, for most of us live in a very stressed society. Consider some of the consequences of the pressure of modern living: thousands of people are taking prescription drugs, and millions of man-hours are lost each year due to sickness; the economic system as a whole faces serious disruption; there is an awful social toll on broken relationships, especially marriages. Medical experts speak with alarm at the cost of stress in an increasingly frenetic world. Many voices are raised offering sound and relevant advice in the management of stress. You may say, 'Thank you; I've read the books and appreciate the advice they offer. I'm even endeavouring to put it into practice, **but** ... that challenging word ... it's not so simple!' There must be more to the answer.

Let us consider the issue from the perspective of personality. The energetic enthusiast, full of vitality, looks with a
mixture of frustration, envy and irritation at the perennially
cool, even-tempered and unruffled individual. 'It's alright
for people like him,' he grumbles. Some people seem more
prone to stress than others, but whatever your nature,
each of us needs to find our pathway to 'the harmonious
working of all the faculties and affections' of which Vine
spoke. Finding it opens the possibility of reaching our full
potential, our promised land. Failing to find it will only
compound our problems, increase our frustrations, and the
stress under which we labour.

I am choleric by nature, going hard on myself and others
in my desire to lead and see results. From school sports
teams and muddy soccer pitches to church youth group
'fun' nights, as a young man I was organising, harassing,
disputing and demanding more effort. You would think it
was the Olympics! I found it hard to live with myself, let
alone to know rest! As a Christian, I was thankful for a godly
foundation to my life and I remember early on having the
inner certainty of having been forgiven, but I knew I was
not at peace with myself.

I took a key step towards finding this peace and living in
rest, when it dawned on me that I was loved by God, who
created me just as I am, gave me all the gifts I needed, and is
determined – through the people and events of my life – to
see that I become the whole person He wants. This aware-
ness immediately destroys the need for comparing myself
with others – life is not a competition between people. No
more 'I wish I was like him,' and 'Why haven't I got her
abilities?' The example of great people urges us towards
excellence, but we need to reach a place of contentment
with how God made us, and use all the skills and abilities at
our disposal to reach our promised land. This is success. In a
stress-filled world, for our health, sanity and satisfaction, we
need to reach a place of rest about who we are. Our natural
gifts should be accepted and developed, not compared with
those of others or complained about.

A different angle will give us a third perspective of the rest

we are seeking. A number of years ago I kept finding myself
challenged by some verses in the Bible which I could not
understand. I knew they held a secret – a key which would
help me unlock the door to a life of active rest. The verses
came from Hebrews 4:

> *'Therefore, since the promise of entering His rest still stands,
> let us be careful that none of you be found to have fallen
> short of it. For we also have had the Gospel preached to us,
> just as they* [the Israelites] *did; but the message they heard
> was of no value to them, because those who heard did not
> combine it with faith. Now we who have believed enter that
> rest ... And yet His* [God's] *work has been finished since the
> creation of the world. For somewhere He has spoken about
> the seventh day in these words: "And on the seventh day
> God rested from all His work" ... There remains, then, a
> Sabbath-rest for the people of God; for anyone who enters
> God's rest also rests from his own work, just as God did from
> His. Let us, therefore, make every effort to enter that rest.'*
> (Hebrews 4:1–4, 9–11)

An easy but somewhat superficial conclusion would be
that everyone needs a weekly day of rest. Even God took a
day off when He had finished creating the universe. Experience has proven the wisdom of the idea; I have maintained
the discipline for myself for a long time. But true rest is
more than a day spent relaxing each week. The context of
the passage warns us against the attitude of the Israelites
and holds two strong lessons: believing what God has
promised and acting on our faith are crucial if we are to
reach our promised land. As a bonus, we are offered the
opportunity of passing the journey in His rest, confident of
the fact that we will arrive and *'enter that rest'*. We are
pilgrims, resting in the promise that the journey will be
completed and that God will keep His promises.

I grappled with this for a long while, sometimes thinking
I had grasped the meaning, sometimes floundering. The
demands of verse 11 sound like more work to find rest: *'Let
us, therefore, make every effort to enter that rest'*! The phrase
'make every effort' ('labour' in some versions of the Bible) is

translated from the Greek word *spoudazo*. We could equally read, *'Let us be diligent to enter that rest.'* How can I rest from my own work? We have already seen this is more than time off, while being diligent to reach this attractive promised land called rest. The passage shows us a people who have escaped slavery in Egypt but who settle for survival in the wilderness, not arriving in their promised land until many years had passed and a generation had died. I don't want that written about you or me.

The Hebrews' passage uses creation as an illustration of the rest God invites us to enter. What are the implications of this? Adam's privileges included headship over creation and being created in God's image and likeness. He was blessed emotionally, socially, morally and spiritually. Has it ever occurred to you that, on the seventh day according to the Genesis account, when Adam woke to his first sunrise, all the aforementioned privileges and blessings were already his? He had not worked for or earned them. Maybe he asked God about the possibility of doing something to help creation along. God could have replied 'Take a day off, Adam; I have finished everything!' So Adam's first full day on earth was a day of rest; in other words, he worked after rest, rather than resting after work.

The rhythm of most people's lives involves rest after work. The creation pattern offers a lifestyle that at a glance may look the same but is in fact radically different. It delivers a rhythm of work after rest. Orthodox Jews still adhere to the principle laid down in the first chapter of the Bible: morning follows evening to make a complete day, rather than *vice versa*. The implication is that we commence our work from a place of refreshment and renewal, as opposed to collapsing into an exhausted heap after our work. Starting work from a place of rest is much more than 'work' after inactivity; it is a **possessional** rest, a realised promise. If we use a different preposition, the statement becomes 'work **in** rest'. Now we have **positional** rest, which is as valuable as possessional rest. It is in me and I am in it!

Just as Adam had all he needed before working, so we also are complete in that which Jesus Christ has purchased for us, and means to us, and wants to deposit in us. From this position and possession I receive great security and confidence. I no longer need be buffeted by the circumstances and events of my life. Rather, I know that I am made in God's image; with Christ living His life in me. I have all the resources necessary to complement the gifts, both natural and spiritual, already given to me. The events of life are being used by God like an anvil and hammer to bring me to maturity and my life to its purpose. God has already planned my life and provided all I need to succeed. He waits for me to believe and have faith in what He has promised, and by the actions of a life of faith to enter and conquer my promised land. To live in the possessional, positional and physical reality of this is to know true rest.

This ground gained, the killer Stress will not stop you. His friend and partner, Striving, will not weary you, and their mutual companion Struggling will never stifle your life by robbing you of your identity, worth and position. I have chosen to live in this rest, and to work from rest, with all my faculties and affections working harmoniously. It is a wonderful place. We looked earlier at some words of Jesus to those who are tired and worn out:

'Walk with me, work with me, watch how I do it.'

That is the best advice possible. As we do what Jesus said, we will learn the unforced rhythms of grace. This sounds good and feels even better. It is worth the diligence necessary to arrive in the promised land of rest.

Chapter 10

All Change!

'I'm resting, and now you are going to challenge me about change? Is life never fair?' But we are pilgrims, learning both to live **in** rest and **with** change. We must disturb the present to embrace the future. A disquiet with the status quo is a necessary ingredient for a better future. This may all sound disturbing. But taking hold of our promised land, reaching our destiny, and arriving at our purpose is disturbing for it demands change. Change nearly always carries a degree of discomfort with it – especially when it is severe or sudden change. But as with the children of Israel, it also offers the promise of better days. They had to learn to trust God in new ways, move to possess their allotted land, put down their roots and defeat giants. We too must leave the comfortable faith of mere 'survival' and move into all that God has planned and desired for us. Many of the things we have already looked at in previous chapters involve change. The way we think, our words and actions – all of them must undergo change if we are to fulfil the potential of our lives.

It has been said that the biggest room in the world is the room for improvement. Change is part of life from dependency in the womb to care of the next generation in maturity. Constant change is here to stay, but most of us resist or avoid it given the opportunity. Mark Twain, with characteristic humour, held that the only person who truly likes change is a wet baby! Yet if we can be honest with ourselves about our level of resistance, we can make the necessary adjustments that will enable us to handle change better.

My son Jonathan and I enjoy expressing different concepts using diagrams. If you find them helpful, enjoy the next paragraph. If you usually don't understand them, you have two options:

1. a chance to change;
2. an opportunity to skip to the next page.

The choice is yours.

The diagram shown in Figure 4 is a house with four rooms, representing four stages that a business can go through. The contention is that a business, at any given time, is in one of four phases: **Renewal**, **Contentment**, **Denial** or **Confusion** – and that it is a one way process. The renewal phase expresses the fact that the business has coped with a major change, broken through and managed it all

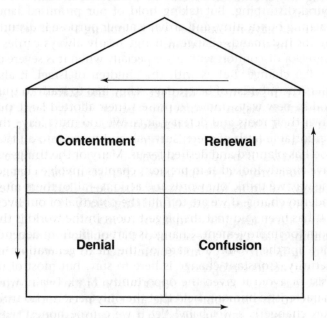

Figure 4

successfully. Flushed with success however, the business can easily become complacent – entering the Contentment phase –failing to see the need for continued effort. This in turn leads to Denial – a definite unwillingness to face the prospect of further change – and eventually to Confusion, where change becomes desperately needed to prevent a further downward spiral.

The same principles may be applied to an individual's life. If you are in Contentment or Denial things are serious; you have left Renewal, but not yet entered a state of Confusion that might force a change. Confusion does not sound appealing, but recognising it as a catalyst to change, and that the right change in a time of confusion will bring you back to renewal, is strong motivation to make the journey. I would contend that our lives as individuals, families and churches go through similar cycles. Learning how to deal with change becomes an important part of living in renewal or success in preference to slavery or survival.

A friend gave me another way of looking at change, this time in the form an equation:

$$A + B + C \geqslant D$$

where A represents a disquiet with the status quo; B represents a vision of something better; C represents the first steps of change, and D represents the cost of change. 'A' people are good at seeing that things aren't what they could or should be. 'B' people are visionaries, and may visualize a better tomorrow. 'C' people have expertise in planning and strategy and know what steps must be taken – but only after the vision has been made clear. Individually 'A'; 'B' or 'C' cannot affect adequate change only when 'A'; 'B' and 'C' are combined can a real assessment of the equation be made. Is there sufficient energy and commitment to overcome the cost and achieve progress?

There is a cost to being a better person or having a better society to live in. Some people are convinced about who Jesus Christ is, and the need to ask for forgiveness. They may accept that it cost Him His life to offer us salvation, but

the real or perceived cost of repentance, and the requirement to change their lifestyle hold them back.

I was reading recently about the international campaign
to release the very poorest nations of the burden of overwhelming national debt. On both sides of the argument,
the $A + B + C$ balance will have to be in place for the cost D,
however it is measured, to be paid – even though there are
compelling arguments that something must be done.

In all the above I urge us to grasp that the efficient and
effective management of change is fundamental to promised land living. If we are to reach our destination and fulfil
the purpose for which we were born then change will a very
necessary part. If you are a church leader reading this book,
then the wise navigation of change – especially on a
corporate level within your own church – is of paramount
importance. Furthermore an appreciation of how people
react to change on a personal level will be beneficial to you.

According to Ralph Neighbour [1] any congregation or
group of people will generally divide into the following
sub-groups: $2\frac{1}{2}$% of the population will be **innovators** or
radicals, ready for a change approximately every four
months. $12\frac{1}{2}$% will be **early-adaptors**, ready for a change
every six to twelve months. 35% are the **early-majority**,
ready for a change every fourteen to twenty-four months.
35% make up the **late-majority**, and will only be prepared
for a change every twenty-four to thirty-six months. $12\frac{1}{2}$%
are **late-adaptors**, accepting change only after a long
'incubation' period of around forty-eight months, and the
remaining $2\frac{1}{2}$% are die-hard traditionalists who generally
refuse to accept any kind of change at all. Give yourself
a little test (see Figure 5), which position best describes
you?

In my life as a preacher and trainer of Christian leaders, I
have observed the practical force of this model. A few years
ago, due to sustained growth, more people were attending
church than our building could comfortably hold. We
considered several solutions to this problem, eventually

[1] *Where Do We Go From Here?*, Ralph W. Neighbour, Touch Publications

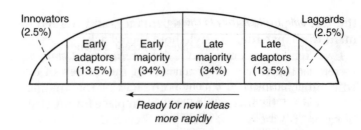

Figure 5   The 'change population'

choosing to use one of the largest halls in our city, despite its limited availability – Sunday afternoons only! This required a drastic change of routine for the congregation. Some, including myself, who had been attending church services on Sunday mornings and evenings all our lives found it a strange and unsettling experience. However, we had prepared the people for change, holding firm to the promise of God that *'the people will be willing in the day of* [God's] *power'* (Psalm 110:3). The move proved to be a great blessing which brought further growth.

Let us apply Neighbour's analysis to the above scenario. One Sunday morning, the leader announces to the congregation that the church can no longer meet in the familiar building. Instead, the services will be held in a larger venue at 2:30 pm. The radicals are excited as they leave the meeting. They encourage the leaders, saying that the project is an answer to prayer. In truth, they have typically prayed little and thought even less about the implications of the change, but they like something new and different. At the other extreme, the traditionalists leave the service in a different way, with a polite 'Good morning', accompanied by a handshake or a gentle embrace. However, they are all wearing a particular expression on their faces which issues a sufficient warning to the leaders of their feelings toward the move. A few days pass before their response filters back. With grave and earnest sincerity, the family head expresses commitment to the church and desire for its success, but after prayer and discussion with 'everyone else', the leaders

Table 1 *Receptivity to change.*

Group	Time taken to accept a change
Innovators	2–4 months
Early adaptors	6 months
Early majority	6–14 months
Late majority	24 months
Late adaptors	36 months
Laggards	48 months

should know that 'everyone' is against the change. The thrust of their statement, though they may not realise it, is 'We don't like change.' Table 1 shows an approximate timescale for the adoption of new ideas by the different groups.

The percentages quoted earlier reflect an average organisation. Thus far in our analysis we have accounted for the attitudes of no more than 30% of the whole church, and possibly as little as 5%. What of the silent majority of people? Be they progressive or conservative in outlook, they are busy with the issues of life, business, family, and service of God through the life of the Church. They are too busy living, giving and serving to waste time complaining! For his or her own peace of mind, any leader must learn that most of the noise and comment comes from the minorities at both ends of the spectrum. If the balance of the group is heavily weighted at either end, the boat will sink. Too many radicals will give a lot of excitement today, but the organisation may not exist tomorrow. With too many traditionalists, the organisation will be dull today and just as ineffective or extinct tomorrow. Developing individual and corporate confidence, clarity of vision and honesty will help us to adjust more easily, and will allow us to effectively reap the many benefits that can follow change.

A better understanding of these principles would help society at every level. Governmental decisions may be poorly received, not because they are inherently bad but because the resistance to change has not been carefully handled. Individuals may not reach their full potential, failing to deal with the emotions and challenges associated with change. Each of us must learn to work with our own personality. Why do some people prepare a detailed route plan prior to any long journey, while others neglect even to check the oil in the car? Why are some early for every event in life, and yet others are invariably late? The answer is that each one of us is created as a unique person with a special blend of ingredients that makes us individuals. Each of us therefore need change to take us from where we truly are to where we want to be. Pretence about our present position will greatly limit the effectiveness of change, and unrealistic expectation about the destination will likewise hinder progress.

Stepping back from these reflections on single instances of change, we will consider now some wider life issues. The very essence and nature of life itself is the ultimate experience of continual change and development. All of us began our lives in total dependency to our mothers, a fact uniquely testified to by our navels! Through our early years we move inexorably towards independence, parts of the process being repeated many times throughout our lives.

Let us use the analogy of a college graduate. Intelligent and well educated, he starts his first job reliant, to an ever-decreasing extent, upon his immediate supervisor, who trains and develops him appropriately. From this state of dependence the graduate matures to a point of counter-dependence, where the supervisor may become equally reliant upon his *protégé*. Following this stage, if not contemporaneous with it, is the state of independence. Eventually the graduate has sufficient experience to leave the company which first employed him and set up his own business. Successful organisations always seek to establish interdependence, where mature and capable people recognise the power of synergy. A group of people working together to achieve the same goal have far greater potential than the same people working independently.

Teamwork is always more efficient and effective than the individual efforts of those who comprise the team. The dilemma facing our graduate is that extended dependence and independence can both prevent him from reaching his potential. Finding the correct balance is an essential part of our pilgrimage. Pride, insecurity and selfishness are hindrances that can prevent us from accepting a team player's role, and are symptoms of unhealthy independence. This is frequently manifested in an unwillingness to be helped by talented companions. Some people hide in dependency from necessary change, or are limited through submitting to domination from a variety of sources.

What can dominate us and why do we allow it? We may be dominated by unhelpful and sinful habits; controlled by the decisions of other family members; limited by the natures of people we work for or with; even overpowered by controlling words, sometimes spoken in false prophecy. All of these work against us to erode our vision and purpose. Knowing before creation that we would choose to rebel against Him, God paid with His Son's life to win back for us the freedom to choose to do right. Having paid such a price, it cannot be God's desire for anyone to be dominated by any circumstance, at any time, be it a habit, family member, political system, or religious ideal. *'It is for freedom that Christ has set us free,'* asserted Paul (Galatians 5:1). Each of us must break out of any domination that is limiting our ability to reach our promised land and live to the full measure of our ability and God's purpose.

Both positive and negative events in our lives may concentrate our minds and catalyse change. At a basic level we can handle the normal rhythms of life, but the developmental changes, which typically carry increased responsibility, are a quite different matter. Sudden change is invariably difficult to manage – divorce, the death of a family member and bankruptcy are painful examples, for which only minimal planning or preparation is usually possible. At the risk of stating the obvious, death is an intrinsic part of life, and the resulting sudden change to friends and relatives, however painful, is unavoidable.

Sudden success or meteoric fame has its own unique challenge. All these are changes, but very different in character; wise people will learn the differences and respond as necessary.

What happens when our lives undergo major change? Let us take a newly married couple as an example, and try to draw out some broad principles. Using the same language as previously, the more radically minded person of the couple will typically be more excited and have higher expectations of this new venture, while the traditionalist is more cautious and commensurately less enthusiastic. In life, things are rarely as good as our highest expectations or as bad as our worst fears, so a period of equalisation or adjustment passes while things settle down and reality sets in. The situation is better than the traditionalist expected, but not quite as rosy as the radical had hoped for. After this initial 'honeymoon' experience, a period of perhaps two years passes – sometimes more, sometimes less – during which the couple regularly confront the challenge of mastering the changes which are all part of a wonderful, romantic marriage! Seeing true reality brings a great release, and confidence increases allowing the couple to deliver their full potential, having grasped the different requirements of their new situation.

Marriage was the specific example chosen, but the principles may be applied with some accuracy to any situation of major change, such as starting a new job, coming to terms with bereavement, or moving to live in a different place. Failure to appreciate the changes that are occurring in and around oneself can prolong the pain, or in the worst-case scenario lead to disaster. In some business establishments, people are promoted very quickly without fully understanding how the operation works. In the extreme, promotion ceases at the point of incompetence – where the person does not possess the necessary gifts and abilities to reach any higher. This is hardly a place of security and fulfilment. Organisations that only promote to the highest levels of leadership from within their own group and culture must take care to maintain high standards of intelligence and competence to avoid this scenario. Sincerity or length of service are never suitable substitutes. The Church could learn a lesson here: if it restricted itself to employing competent and called people, the need to move them quickly, often for damage limitation purposes, would largely be avoided.

I trust that as we consider our character and make our way from dependence to inter-dependence, the challenge of change in cycles and uncertainties will find us prepared. If we fail to embrace change, our promised land will remain beyond our reach. We may fall, but we must rise. The Bible promises us that:

> 'The path of the righteous is like the first gleam of dawn, shining ever brighter till the full light of day.'
>
> (Proverbs 4:18)

The unknown may be daunting, the changes ahead may be challenging, but perseverance will yield the promised land of fulfilled potential. Then with Paul we will one day be able to say,

> 'I have fought the good fight, I have finished the race, I have kept the faith.'
>
> (2 Timothy 4:7)

Chapter 11

Training and Planning

I was recently confronted by a difficult leadership situation in another country. Wisdom was needed to avoid the damage which may be inflicted on individuals, communities and churches during a time of crisis. Dorothy Ann, my wife, felt impressed to encourage me to be: clear, concise and careful. It was good advice. While prayer is vital during such times, my experience has been that training, planning and preparation are also important ingredients if the crisis is to be successfully negotiated and its effects minimised.

Someone has said,

> 'People's lives are limited by a compass of: compromise, indecision, past-thinking and lack of vision.'

If there is any truth in these comments, then we must take action, drastic action if necessary, to break the limitation. Training, planning and preparing ourselves, will prove vital links in the breakthrough process. Paul teaches Timothy to *'train yourself to be godly'* (1 Timothy 4:7). The original language indicates nakedness, being stripped of outer clothing. It infers the picture of the gymnast, prepared in mind and body, able to perform the routines of their sport. Paul is exhorting us to train with the discipline of a gymnast.

If we accept the challenge of the quotation above, we must rigorously apply ourselves to ending compromise in our lives. Compromise may come through lacking a full understanding of the truth, fear of people's opinions or simply our insecurity. Whatever causes inappropriate compromise must be faced up to and trained out of us. The same can be said about the double-mindedness that so often accompanies indecision, whether driven by a fear of failure or a simple lack of experience in making decisions. I have met many intelligent, educated young people who find themselves leaving university, unprepared for the future, having been over-sheltered from any serious decision making. I have already written about the need to mind our own business in the business of our minds. The habits and inaccuracies of our thought life can dangerously circumscribe our lives. Work is done in many business corporations specifically to address the imbalance of time spent on things that are in the past, when all possibilities for development and advance lie in the future. There needs to be less time spent reading the minutes of meetings and more time spent strategizing for the future and developing vision. Similarly, the view we as individuals have of our past, and the amount of time we spend thinking about it, greatly limits our future. Some of the change–management experts say that we spend as much as 80% of our time focusing on the past, 15% on the present, and only 5% on the future. An example may be the time we spend musing over anecdotes. Yet we are urged to:

> 'Forget the former things; do not to dwell on the past. See, I am doing a new thing!'   (Isaiah 43:18, 19)

The 'present' constitutes the 'action' part of our lives and we must surely learn to make the most of every opportunity. The reactive use of today and the reflective application of yesterday, although sometimes appropriate, should more often be turned into anticipation, planning, prayer, thinking and even dreaming about the future. All our possibilities are today and tomorrow! We must arrest some of the 95% of our lives spent on the past and present, and better use that energy on the future. The fourth observation of the quotation we are looking at states that lack of vision limits our lives. I have already written about the need to truly 'see'. My emphasis here is to illustrate that in all these areas of our lives we need to apply training, discipline and hard work if – as God intended – we are to fully reach our potential and live in our promised land.

My late friend Bob Gordon spoke of a multitude of training methods in his manual *Master Builders*. These included one-to-one training, apprenticeship, expert help, observation, conferences, workshops and seminars, retreats, evening Bible school, in-service training, use of libraries and correspondence courses. All these need a commitment on our part to *'train to be godly.'* What do I explicitly mean? In my speech, love, motivation, faith and trust, I must learn to devote (1 Timothy 4:13), not neglect (4:14) be diligent (4:15) give wholly (4:15), watch closely (4:16) and persevere (4:16) in wholehearted good actions. The Apostle Peter would also add the word 'prepare' – literally 'to gird up your loins for energetic action'. You will not see the full fruit instantly when your mind and actions are brought under the control of Christ, but the fruit of a trained life will grow! We must change our 'I want' attitude to an 'I will' one, realizing, as with most things in life, that short-term pain (discipline) means long-term gain.

I recently heard the background to the remarkable success enjoyed by Linford Christie, the British, 100-metre sprinter. Until his late twenties, Christie was a journeyman athlete, with a London team. A new trainer saw his potential, helped him focus on his athletics and fitness, and watched him become a world-beater. The training was arduous and did not yield results for a long time until suddenly one day he ran the distance three tenths of a second faster than ever before – a significant improvement. His training had paid off. So will yours. The result is that we learn to be faithful both in season and out of season, when we feel like it and when we don't. These disciplines make champions in the world of sports, arts and business and they will also help us to possess our promised land.

Each of us has a responsibility for our own development. We also must remember that in many situations in life we have not succeeded until we are succeeded. By this I mean that a true visionary will never self-indulgently protect his vision; others will feed on his enthusiasm so that whatever great work he is about, will be perpetuated. The developing, discipling and training of others is challenging but necessary work. You must not wait until you are mature, polished or accomplished before you invest in other people. Timothy was inspired to share what he had heard from Paul with other reliable men who in turn would teach still others (2 Timothy 2:2). Part of your own development is to invest in others. The process will make you a better person. Humbly share who you are and what you know and you will be trained even as you train others.

Many Christian leaders think that all most people lack is sound teaching, but Jesus' teaching was an essential part of a wider disciple-making process, and He urges us to, *'go and make disciples of all nations...'* (Matthew 28:19). Be encouraged in this; it is hard but satisfying work. You will pass through times of disappointment. Jesus had His Judas, and most of the men who had spent years travelling with Him, watching Him, and listening to His message, let Him down at His time of crisis. Later, however, they turned the world upside down in the power of Pentecost. The power of Pentecost is still available; much joy awaits those who will invest their lives in training and discipling others. So we must train ourselves, train others, then together with others see the power of synergy work for the greater good. Two are better than one; together we can do what we could not do alone.

A few years ago I became conscious of God's voice redirecting the use of my time and energy. Many conversations and musings culminated in three significant statements. I was urged to spend the next part of my life focusing on where I could build rather than bless, on what would be significant rather than that which appears to be successful and on what is important and not just urgent. Some people do not understand that it is appropriate to control the planning and time-tabling of your days, pacing your life wisely rather than being driven by the urgent demands of what others think should be the priorities of your life. To do this properly requires an openness to the over-ruling providence of a loving Father. The Proverbs express the truth succinctly:

> *'Many are the plans of a man's heart, but it is the Lord's purpose that prevails.'* (Proverbs 19:21)

We speak of God as having divine foresight, but the Bible also shows God as our provider:

> *'The Lord is my shepherd, I shall not be in want.'*
> (Psalm 23)

To provide means to make due preparation, and that requires planning. The promise of our salvation, the many deliverers He engineered for His people, and the timing of the day of Pentecost – all were products of the Creator's master plan. God is a God who plans. He knows the end from the beginning, and does not have to adjust His plans through the use of hindsight, learning from His mistakes, because He doesn't make mistakes.

The question posed by Stephen in Acts 7:49, has often challenged me:

> *'What kind of house will you build for me? Says the Lord.'*

At various times it has meant the 'house' of my own life, or the development of my family, church community or nation. Jesus illustrates the need for planning when talking about the cost of becoming a disciple. He says,

> *'Suppose one of you wants to build a tower. Will he not first sit down and estimate the cost to see if he has enough money to complete it? For if he lays the foundation and is not able to finish it, everyone who sees it will ridicule him, saying, "this fellow began to build and was not able to finish."'*
> (Luke 14:28–30)

Similarly, if you are to build a successful 'house' – whatever that means for you at this moment – some important things must be put in place and understood. What are you building on? What is your foundation? What are you building with? What are you building for? Above all, you must come to a realization of your God-ordained purpose. If your life is not built on the foundation of Jesus as the rock and strengthened by a continuing obedience to His instruction, then your house like many before it, however well intentioned, will fall down. I will not amplify these truths in detail. I wish simply to underline the point that proper planning is a prerequisite of successful living. Before leaving the illustration however, allow me one further comment. If the Church of Jesus is to be successfully built in any generation, we must, without regard to denominational politics or dispensational niceties, build the way He instructed us. Christ Jesus is the great foundation – the cornerstone, the essential element. The ministry gifts, especially that of the Apostle and Prophet, are also a foundational requirement. The aim of 'church' is that a whole body of believing people is to be brought to maturity and everyone is to use their gifts in service for Christ. This sort of church will be filled with the glory of God and motivated to touch their world with the immeasurable love of God.

John the Baptist was sent to prepare the way of the Lord. The same Spirit of Elijah that Jesus said was in John and his ministry, is in the earth today, still preparing the way of the Lord. A great Hosanna of praise circles the earth every day, as millions of people in the multitude of nations praise the God of Glory, Father, Son and Holy Spirit, and raise a Hosanna, saying *'Blessed is He who comes in the name of the Lord.'* The Church, under the baton of Holy Spirit – the great conductor, who delights to make Jesus more visible, loved and understood – is singing its anthems to Messiah, the King of Kings, whose physical body left the earth nearly 2000 years ago and who one-day, I pray soon, will again be physically visible. Every eye will see Him and every tongue will confess that 'Jesus is Lord'. God's plans are in hand. He has never been late for an appointment in all of human history. Until that great day when the earth shall again be filled with the Glory of the Lord, let us with diligence plan and prepare.

The golden rule in all of our planning must be that the structures we create should not overpower the life they are in place to sustain. Our eyes must be clear and our hearts on fire for the purpose of God in our lives. Planning and training will help us enter the fullness of our promised land, becoming all that God intends us to be, possessing all that He intends us to possess, until the fullness of His plan is unveiled at the glorious return of Jesus, the Christ our Saviour and Lord.

Chapter 12

Unity and Humility

The Bible, our guide book to promised land living, instructs us that if we humble ourselves we will be exalted, but it also warns that if we exalt ourselves we will be humbled. God hates pride and resists those who are proud. For successful promised land living we have more personal work to do. It is humbling ourselves. It is not the sham of merely religious behaviour, nor the kind of false modesty that is unable to accept a compliment, but a true humbling of ourselves before the Lord (James 4:10).

Many times in these chapters we have returned to the example of Jesus Christ as our model and source of life. Without Him the promised land, as God designed it, stays out of our reach. But when our lives are lived out in commitment to Him, new horizons fill our field of vision. Toward the end of His ministry, with the daunting shadow of the cross coming ever closer, Jesus provided us with a classic illustration of His humility, and with it some keys which we would do well to appropriate. The evening meal was being served and the desperate deeds of treachery were fermenting in Judas the betrayer. Jesus was very conscious of the importance of these events, His mind *'knowing that the time had come for Him to leave this world'* (John 13:1). He removed His outer clothing, wrapped a towel around His waist, poured water into a basin and washed His disciples' feet, drying them with the towel.

A simple scene. With good reason. Jesus was doing the work normally reserved for a servant. His behaviour provoked a reaction. The washing over, He dressed and returned to His seat. In the teaching that followed, He revealed a secret to promised land living:

> *'Now that you know these things, you will be blessed if you do them.'*

What He has displayed here is not some grovelling weakness, but He reveals Himself as a man who knows who He is, the power He has been given, where He came from, where He is going, and the high regard in which the disciples hold Him. These I believe can be defined as the essential ingredients necessary for genuine humility. Jesus was supremely confident about His status and His mission. He was able to say He was their teacher and also their Lord, a very unusual claim. *'The one occupying the supreme place'*, my study Bible says. 'Master,' 'owner,' 'sir,' and 'one having authority' are alternative meanings. From this place of security, serving was easy! In case this language is too bold for you, let me quote the first three verses of the story in full:

> *'It was just before the Passover Feast. Jesus knew that the time had come for Him to leave this world and go to the Father. Having loved His own who were in the world, He now showed them the full extent of His love. The evening meal was being served, and the devil had already prompted Judas Iscariot, son of Simon, to betray Jesus. Jesus knew that the father had put all things under His power, and that He had come from God and was returning to God.'*   (John 1:1–3)

He knew who he was, where He had come from and where He was going.

Are you confident of your status and your mission? Do you know where you came from and where you are going? How do you handle other people's recognition of your gift? Some delight in rehearsing that we are miserable sinners (and who can argue with that?). Others remind us of Isaiah's language *'Fear not, thou worm Jacob'* (Isaiah 41:14 AV), often forgetting that the same chapter says that we are chosen servants (41:9). Here is one of those paradoxical truths: we are sinners, left to ourselves we are capable of unimaginable things; but it is also true that we are special, precious individuals, uniquely created by God and loved by Him. God is committed to our success, we are the 'apple of His eye' and He has gone to extraordinary lengths to make His passion and love for us visible and attainable.

We need a revelation to understand who we are, the sons of God, then humbly accept that everything good in us and our lives has come from Him. It is easy then to be 'low before God', the simplest spiritual meaning of the word humble. Serving others, as Jesus illustrated, is not difficult from this position of security.

I have mentioned elsewhere that Jesus never allowed Himself to be trapped by other people's thinking or confessions. He was not afraid of guilt by association. He knew who He was. If the charismatic churches, and especially the groups labelled Classic Pentecostals, are to take their place in today's world, they have an obligation to deal with their many insecurities and obsessions. Some come from historic rejection by all the main line Christian groups earlier in the twentieth Century. Others come from a position of insecurity about their background, having had limited scholarship, inadequate resources or incomplete applications of truth. These are a few of the giants which must be beaten. Genuine humility serves from a position of confidence in who we are and what God has made us. Phillips Brooks, author of the carol 'O Little Town of Bethlehem' said of humility:

> 'The true way to be humble is not to stoop until you are smaller than yourself, but to stand at your real height against some higher nature that will show you what the real smallness of your greatness is.'

The world of selling and self-improvement is full of language about taking control within, imagining yourself a success, dressing, thinking, speaking and acting successfully; wearing the right colors and clothes. We are told we must believe in ourselves. All this and a myriad of other words and ideas (I mention these only to illustrate my point), will help us to make a good living, but will they make a good life? A wealthy friend of mine stands in front of the mirror each morning and speaks words of acceptance and 'prophesies' his success. Others, who learn this part of his secret, may copy his technique. However, behind this confident confession is a Christian man who knows that all he has achieved has involved hard work, a bit of genius and the use of his own and other people's gifts. His ultimate security is not in his success or status as a businessman, but as a sinner loved and befriended, forgiven and accepted by God. Knowing who he is as a son of God, a man of destiny, he can apply positive words and attitudes to his daily life, and enjoy the success God has given him. This may be a different view of humility than is often taught, but I believe it is a legitimate part of successful living in the promised land.

The servant mentality that so easily flows out of humility, makes it so much simpler to be other-centred. *'Each of you should look not only to your own interests, but also to the interests of others'* (Philippians 2:4), is Paul's injunction to the Philippian Christians. He immediately links the thought to Jesus,

> *'Your attitude should be the same as that of Christ Jesus.'*
> (Philippians 2:5)

Later in the same chapter he speaks in glowing terms about Timothy but adds this challenging rider:

> *'I have no one else like him, who takes a genuine interest in your welfare. For everyone looks out for his own interests, not those of Jesus Christ.'* (Philippians 2:20–21)

How sad, but unfortunately still too often true. The unity necessary to fully occupy the land does not flourish in the soil of self-interest.

'By uniting we stand, by dividing we fall.' So say the words of an eighteenth-century song (*The Liberty Song*, 1768). The Bible psalmist wrote that where the people dwell in unity, God commands the blessing (Psalm 133). Further back in history, the Bible records God's conclusion to the ideas of building the tower of Babel.

> *'The Lord said "If as one people speaking the same language they have begun to do this, then nothing they plan to do will be impossible for them."'* (Genesis 11:6)

The people had a commitment to work on a goal, maintain effective communications and stay united. This momentary trip across history reminds us of something we all know; power, strength and amazing possibilities lie together in unity.

In the illustration which I have threaded through this book, the nation of Israel all suffered together, left Egypt together, crossed the Red Sea together, moved around the wilderness and later walked round Jericho together. Different groups within the nation had their own unique functions, but they stayed together through the good times and the bad. When the land was finally allocated, those who had already inherited their family and tribal lot were instructed to continue the invasion and fight alongside the other tribes until each received their promised land.

What about unity today? We live in an age of moral bankruptcy. In a 'good' church, those who fall may be disciplined in loving righteousness. But how often people will forsake the 'unity' of the local church after such an experience and decide to leave quietly to join another group of Christians elsewhere – no questions asked; no inquiry made. Groups of Christians with strong views about some facet of doctrine, or a particular outreach burden are viewed with suspicion by other groups, or themselves judge others for their perceived shortcomings. And so the merry-go-round continues. Many new church groups born out of frustration and division, struggle gainfully but with little success. How you leave any situation in life will affect the way in which you enter the next. Why does the Church of Jesus allow itself so much fragmentation, dishonoring rather than honoring, and consequently rendering our work much less effective than it should be?

In my own city, an envisioned few have persisted for

many years in gathering people together, chiefly to pray, from many different church traditions. It has sometimes been hard work, but thankfully more often rewarding and joyful. Hundreds of people are now involved, praying for the key components of our city life. The fruit of such unity is visible at present but will be much more noticeable in the future.

Unity starts much further back in the cycle of our life than I have been expressing. We must first unite our lives to the purpose and plan of our Creator and Saviour or we will struggle to make any true harmony out of our human existence. Peace with God and submission to His Lordship and authority will release a stream of benefits into every part of our life. These benefits will enable us to function properly in our relationship with other people – family, friends, work and leisure colleagues, even those we may dislike!

Disease in the human body can be limited by a life in harmony and at peace. Doctors attribute much sickness to psychosomatic origins. Relational breakdown is one of the most awful curses of life today, damaging so many people, adults and children, with the tragic trauma of rejection. Much of this discord could be avoided if more people lived humble and united lives. Wherever you look, national or local government, education or health care, on a macroscopic or the microscopic, unity and teamwork, harnessing other skills, doing things together, will always provide benefit and improvement. We who are involved will also 'feel better'. It seems so right to help, support and unite for the common good.

'Uniting we stand, dividing we fall' are the simple words of the old song. Wherever the challenge of this chapter speaks to you, respond positively. My prediction is that embracing new levels of humility and unity will quicken our pace, allowing us to cover the ground more quickly on our way to and through the promised land.

Chapter 13

Breakthrough!

From time to time, news filters out of a pharmaceutical laboratory concerning a life-saving wonder drug. It heralds a breakthrough in the treatment of some deadly disease. The value of a manufacturer's shares suddenly rocket on the rumour of a breakthrough in technology. In a third scenario, after patient diplomacy the opponents in a long running dispute are persuaded to dialogue instead of fight, and newspaper headlines scream 'Breakthrough!'

The Israelites, whose history we have been considering, needed to break through many physical, psychological and spiritual barriers in their transition from slavery, through survival and into success. After the trauma of leaving slavery and survival, their success in the Promised Land required multiple breakthroughs! The book of Joshua records the early part of the saga, cataloguing the plans, successes, challenges and failures. Particularly instructive to us, however, are the attitudes shown by Joshua himself, and his fellow octogenarian, Caleb.

The Lord had said to Joshua,

> 'You are very old, and there are still very large areas of land to be taken over.'   (Joshua 13:1)

Instead of whimpering about the size of the task and asking for early retirement, Joshua prepares a plan of action and confronts the nation:

> *'How long will you wait before you begin to take possession*
> *of the land that the Lord, the God of your fathers, has given*
> *you?'*   (Joshua 18:3)

The challenge behind the question applies to every human being. Are you content that you have reached your potential? Has God made you promises which as yet are unfulfilled? Are there goals which you have yet to attain? If the answer is 'Yes,' then, like me, you need more breakthroughs.

The key point of any breakthrough is in the mind:

> Sow a thought, reap an action. Sow an action, reap a habit.
> Sow a habit, reap a character. Sow a character, reap a destiny.

At 85 years old, Caleb approached Joshua to request his inheritance (Joshua 14:6–13). He had obviously formed a habit of breaking through against the attitude of, 'I'm too old for that now.' Instead, he remembered the promise of God delivered by Moses the man of God, and simply believed it. The effect of this habit was to shape his character, which in turn formed his destiny. Overshadowing all these events is the promise of God which brings light to the great unknown:

> *'... [Follow the ark of the covenant] Then you will know*
> *which way to go, since you have never been this way before.'*
>   (Joshua 3:4)

Christians have a responsibility to possess for themselves what has already been paid for. The good news we've grasped is more than Jesus dying to take away our sin. Jesus brings again the blessings and privileges that God had intended humanity to enjoy but were diverted by sin. Having given us Christ, the Bible insists that with Him we have been freely given all things. It is therefore time to break through the barriers of thinking 'I can't,' 'I don't deserve it,' 'I'm not good enough.' If anything in life has already been paid for, collection and possession is required, not further payment. This principle always works. If the power that holds people in addiction, fear or phobia has been broken by Christ's death and resurrection, why stay a slave to something from which you long to be free? Why pay again for what has already been paid for?

In the face of this offer, so many people say 'Mañana – tomorrow. I'll deal with it tomorrow.' One lady I remember spent fourteen years addicted to tobacco. Another required sleeping pills every day for thirteen years. A continental friend spent many years gambling his nights away. Fear limits many people in various ways: fear of the dark, of open spaces, of lifts, of flying, of dying – the list goes on. All the people I mentioned above finally arrived at a day like today when each realised that the power to be free was available to them. They each broke through to a new level in their lives, conquering addiction, fear and phobia. The same possibility is open for everyone, whatever their situation. Remember, your freedom has been paid for. Each of us can break through to receive it.

There is more to discover in understanding the power of breakthrough. Not only should we possess what has been paid for; we need also to progress into that which has been promised, and prepare for what has already been planned for us. Consider young David the shepherd, who was shown preference over all his older brothers at the time of his anointing by Samuel (1 Samuel 16). This anointing was the beginning of the many exciting, difficult and demanding experiences which David had to go through before he was finally anointed as Israel's king. It is not enough to have the promise or the anointing alone; they are key points of recognition, confirmation or comfort, but they are not the journey itself. To reach our destinies, we must make the journey, progress and be pilgrims.

Along the journey, from receipt of the anointing and the promise, we experience the Four-A principle:

All Anointed people Attract Attention;

and its three-A consequence:

All Anointed people get Attacked.

In 2 Samuel 5, his enemies heard that David had been anointed king and decide to attack him. His enemies call the place of the battle 'The Valley of Giants', while David calls it 'The Lord breaks out'. On the journey to reach your potential, expect God to turn your place of serious opposition into the place of breakthrough. The experience is not exclusive to David. All anointed leaders, everyone with potential for excellence, and all who would achieve their purpose and possess their promised land, must pass through the Valley of Giants and win!

Let us seek to apply the principles we have observed to our own lives. Many members of the human race accept their given level of existence, relationship or prosperity, and refuse to cross the pain barrier that accompanies breakthrough to a new level in life. How then can we live life today, so that by its end we will be further into our personal land of promise? Astronomers tell us that there are many black holes in outer space, collapsed stars with gravitational fields strong enough to bend light. Yet the human eye can see that space is filled with bright stars. This serves as a useful model for life. Let me explain.

Each of us, whoever, wherever and whatever we are, stand today as the product of our birth, training, experience and gifts. We cannot alter any of these historic facts; the time has expired for that. We can choose to use our gifts differently, gain further experience or be involved in alternative training from today, but we cannot change what is fact. We can change our name, live in a different place, and pretend things did not happen – with a measure of success! However, if we are to truly approach our full potential and purpose, we must come to terms with the good and the bad, the blessings and curses of our birth, training, experience and gifts.

I must confess enthusiasm for my Christian faith and convictions. Without belief in an Almighty God who is in total, ultimate control of the universe, we are left to flounder in the morass of relativism prescribed by psychology, mental gymnastics, New Age religion or devil worship. Even in the face of the most extreme human suffering, I have unshakeable confidence in the power of the Christian Gospel. As the epitome of His creation, God gave mankind various freedoms, most pertinently the freedom of choice. A corollary to this freedom is that the consequence of wrong or bad choices must be borne by someone – on occasions, the victim is apparently innocent. It has been said that sin will always cost more than you want to pay, take you further than you want to go, and keep you longer than you want to stay. In the face of this, the Gospel insists that whatever we have done and whatever has happened to us, the price paid by Jesus Christ in His death on the cross is sufficient. With His subsequent resurrection, His death is evidence of the transcendent nature of God converging with His immanence. The all-powerful God took our place as a man to break the power of sin, and to make the offer that through His resurrection life the penalty, power and damage of our own or other's past mistakes can be erased. We are freely offered a new start.

This confidence is vital if we are to focus on the bright stars of our future and not the black holes of our past, which can suck the life from our present and future. Let us consider birth, the first category of the four I mentioned. Some people are born into privilege, others into poverty. Some are born into loving homes, others are deserted. Some are nurtured, others neglected. All the circumstances of your birth, family and early life will have powerfully shaped the person you are today. You may say 'I am still unloved and unwanted, I was born illegitimate and unplanned. Why did I have no father?' The negative side of such questions can indicate black holes in a person's life. Your early years may, like mine, have been very secure. All of us must break through any limitation that stems from our early years. You may be living with the burden of family expectations; born into a banking family, are you expected to follow the family line? Allowing yourself to be conformed to other people's plans can drain you dry of the potential God has placed within you. Your family disciplines and traditions all have their place, but none should hinder you from achieving God's purpose for your life.

What about the training, the education you received? Confidence or complaint about this area of your past can be either a black hole or a bright star for you. A poor education may spur you on to improve yourself, or it may prejudice you against education. Confidence at the quality of your education or training may either inspire you to share your knowledge, teaching others, or it may generate niggling fears and insecurities when confronted with questions to which you do not know the answers. As for the experiences you may have had in your life, whether painful or pleasant, they all have the potential to be stumbling stones into black holes or stepping stones into bright stars.

Now the fourth part: your gifts and abilities, the natural and spiritual deposits that contribute to making you the person you are. "Why can't I earn as much as X? Why can't I sing as well as Y? Why am I less attractive than Z?' This is the language of comparison and discontent. The feeling behind these questions is resentment towards who we are and how God made us. In His infinitely grand plan, He made you the person you are and has given you all the gifts you need to fulfil His purpose. Our responsibility is not to compare ourselves with others but to develop and refine that which God has given us. Both contentment and arrival at our destiny lie down this pathway.

Vast quantities of money, time and energy are dissipated in servicing these insatiable black holes. Each has its own name: 'Why me?' 'What if...?' 'If only...' The effort to which people will go in order to gain approval and acceptance amongst their peers is remarkable. Flamboyant actions or attitudes, expensive lifestyle, aggressive or anti-social behaviour: all speak volumes about someone's personal black hole. Insecurities about one's background, abilities, education and experience – all have the potential to place huge demands upon finances, time and effort. The root of the problem is man's non-acceptance of himself. Millions of people the world over, Christian and non-Christian, are spending their lives feeding black holes, unaware that everything should be different. The promised land can never be fully enjoyed unless we finally fill the black holes and turn to the future with its bright stars. But how?

First, appropriate for yourself the finished work of the cross of Jesus against all sin, failure, rejection and insecurity – every known and unknown black hole. Then actively refuse every accusation that tries to focus your attention on the black hole questions. Consider the promises of God about your future:

> *'He who began a good work in you will carry it on to completion.'* (Philippians 1:6)

> *'From the beginning God chose you to be saved through the sanctifying work of the Spirit and through belief in the truth. He called you to this through our Gospel, that you might share in the glory of our Lord Jesus Christ.'*
> (2 Thessalonians 2:13–14)

> *'For we are God's workmanship, created in Christ Jesus to do good works, which God prepared in advance for us to do.'*
> (Ephesians 2:10)

The Bible is full of such hope and faith-inspiring truths. Read it every day – it is speaking about you!

Next, invest your money, time and energy in developing your future. Winners sacrifice today for tomorrow, whilst losers sacrifice tomorrow for today. You were not called to be average, the top of the bottom, the best of the worst. You were called to live in your promised land, achieve your potential, reach your goals and live to purpose. You can appropriate this today. The sooner you do so, the quicker you can look back without fear and enjoy the widening future of your goals, destiny and purpose. Recall what Joshua said to the people:

> *'How long will you wait before you begin to take possession of the land that the Lord, the God of your fathers, has given you?'* (Joshua 18:3)

I ask you the same question: 'How long will you wait?' No evil or awful thing that has ever happened to you, no enjoyable or successful time in any of your yesterdays –

nothing need limit your future. Through His birth, life, training, experience, death, resurrection and gifts the living Son of God offers you the opportunity to break through, turning your black holes to bright stars. Why wait any longer? It's time for a new breakthrough – out of the valley of giants to the place where God breaks through!

For those who enjoy things expressed diagrammatically, the same teaching is shown in Figure 6.

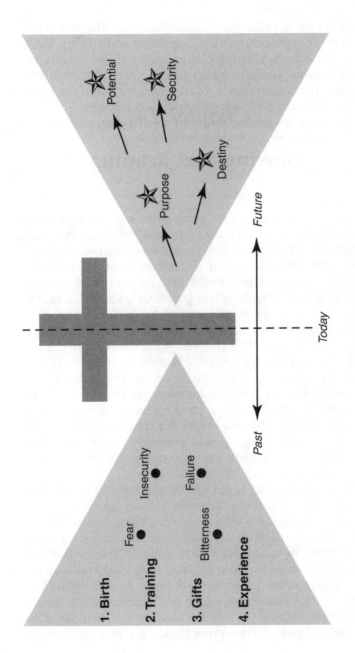

Figure 6   Black holes and bright stars

Chapter 14

Sowing and Reaping

Late one night, travelling home with my family, I drove past an anxious-looking man who was waving a petrol can. My family all sang out, 'You should have stopped and given him a lift!' They were right, so back we went. We took him first to a petrol station to fill his can, and then returned him to his car. I think he was grateful. He seemed to be, but that is not of great importance to me. It is of more importance to him if he is to benefit from the principle we're looking at in this chapter. What mattered to me was that I sowed the right seed. I reaped the rewards of this recently when, on the evening of an important family occasion, my son's car broke down as he was returning from Birmingham. All that was necessary was a phone call to a dear friend who said, 'Leave it to me. You have enough to think about tonight,' and promptly sorted the whole thing out. The problem was solved, and the whole family were present to enjoy the special evening.

What do you like to get out of life? Do you enjoy other people speaking encouragement to you, getting a sweet smile, receiving help with a problem, being trusted? Whatever it is, whether in relationships, business and commerce, hospitality, or in any other field, you would do well to sow what you would like to reap. 'You reap what you sow' is a law that reaches every part of life – it isn't limited to agriculture. Consider for a moment: a farmer plants wheat, expecting to reap ... wheat. Imagine his surprise if he received a bountiful harvest of apples! The idea is ridiculous.

If you exercise any form of generosity, don't be surprised if people are generous to you – that is reaping. If you have been shouting at employees and relatives for years, you had better make a quick change, say sorry and sow some different seeds. When you smile, you receive many a warm smile in response. All our thoughts, words and actions reap their own rewards.

Some seeds grow quickly with early returns, while others take years to come to maturity. Many years ago, some friends of mine helped a young lady who was struggling to pay some outstanding bills. The years passed, and they entirely forgot about the incident. Three years ago they were travelling in Scandinavia. Walking out of Oslo International Airport, my friends heard someone shouting their names, and turned to be greeted by a very smart lady. 'I heard you were coming here! You must stay with me. I will drive you anywhere you need to go. I really want to look after you; you were so kind to me!' My friends had long forgotten, but the young lady they had helped remembered. Now much more prosperous, she wanted to say thank you to them. It was time for them to reap.

I once sat with a Christian man in Singapore who told me the remarkable history of his part in running a Christian mission. He rehearsed many stories of miraculous provision to me, repeatedly telling me that it was always time to sow. Whenever resources became limited he would immediately support some other missionary work with sacrificial giving, continually proving God's faithfulness in this law of sowing and reaping. Living this way takes faith, but the law remains: **what you sow is what you reap**. A short time of sacrifice, with faith, can bring huge returns.

To illustrate the principle further, consider this story. A small group of Indians had survived, year by year, on a simple formula: in the sowing season they would plant one bag of grain and reap ten bags at harvest time. Nine of the ten bags were used for food throughout the year, with the remaining bag being saved to begin the process all over again the following year. A missionary had lived with the group for some years, and having gained their confidence he now made a challenging suggestion. 'Let us live very frugally this year on only eight bags of grain, but let us cultivate more ground, planting two bags.' The leaders agreed, and everyone ate a little less. The two bags of grain produced twenty bags, and everyone was happy to return to eating nine bags a year, leaving eleven bags to sow the following year. Eleven bags of grain produced one hundred and ten bags; now the group could live extravagantly on ten bags, cultivate much more ground, and plant one hundred bags. The next harvest was a thousand bags of grain. So after only three years, everything had changed. The yearly cycle of survival had been broken. The tribe could eat more than previously; they had one hundred bags to grow and nine hundred bags to sell, giving them the option of many other improvements. The cost of breaking the survival programme was one year of careful eating. The benefits all came from sowing just one extra bag of grain.

Every good investment will bring its return. Many individuals and families – to say nothing of church organisations – live from hand to mouth. They have nothing to invest (so they think) and therefore receive no harvest. This is a question of vision and imagination: anyone can invest in education and training, spend time helping others, plan the better usage of their financial resources, or any number of other actions in order to sow.

The promised land does not promise hand-outs and easy options. God says it is a good land, and that He is watching over it, but to what end? With regard to the topic in hand, He is watching to ensure that the law of sowing and reaping is properly administered and fulfilled. Both sides of the principle are attested to with words of wisdom.

> 'He who sows righteousness reaps a sure reward.'
> (Proverbs 11:18)

> 'He who sows wickedness reaps trouble.'   (Proverbs 22:8)

Paul expresses the same truth when he says,

> 'God cannot be mocked. A man reaps what he sows.'
> (Galatians 6:7)

In writing to the Macedonian Christians who had begun to live by these principles, he said,

> *'Remember this, whoever sows sparingly will also reap sparingly, and whoever sows generously will also reap generously.'*   (2 Corinthians 9:6)

With specific regard to material blessings and increased finance, we must remember Paul's further injunction:

> *'You will be made rich in every way so that you can be generous on every occasion and through us your generosity will result in thanksgiving to God.'*   (2 Corinthians 9:11)

These principles are meant to defend us from the two extremes of a self-indulgent attitude and the poverty mentality of millions of people on every continent.

What of the challenge to those who, for whatever reason, are enjoying any form of abundance, who possess and are receiving much more than they need? It must be time for wise, large-scale investments again. The law will keep working. Part of your investment should be directly into God's work through the local church and its missions programme. Everyone would be well advised to give at least ten per cent of their yearly income and profits. It is an investment that will be blessed. Some of the wise Christian philanthropists of past generations started at this amount and ended giving much higher proportions of their wealth. God made His law work, and they had more than enough. Many wise people know how well this works in business, commerce and industry – the principle given is 'speculate to accumulate'. Out of thankfulness for your success, you honour God; in anticipation, you express thanks to God who gives you breath, energy and ideas. He tells us, *'Test me in this'* (Malachi 3:10). In other words, give Him at least this ten per cent tithe and see what happens!

This law extends much further than money and the trappings of modern living – after all, it worked for the Israelites in the promised land, and they had no cookers, washing machines or televisions there. The law relates to love and kindness, friendship and service; everything, every relationship and every circumstance in life. I am often invited to speak at different venues in my own country and abroad. There is no shortage of people to accompany me. I delight in the company of my wife or other family members, but this is not always possible. Why should I have so many offers to be accompanied or driven around when I travel? In part, I believe it is because many years ago I loved the privilege of serving the servants of God. Many people see only the reaping part of the cycle and fail to look for signs of sowing earlier in the sequence. This will almost invariably provide insight to the reaping time in a person's life.

It is a sobering thought that the negative is also true. When the harvest is one of bad attitudes, lack of co-operation and continuing difficulty, one of the possibilities is negative seed sown in days gone by. What must be done? Staying with the agricultural metaphor, the best plan is to change the seed you're sowing while praying for crop failure on what you've already done! Discipline yourself to co-operate with people when they ask for help. Actively seek out opportunities to be useful to others. Check your reaction in crisis or confrontational situations. Practise generosity, of every variety, in every circumstance, with all sorts of people. But be warned – you will only achieve the greatest benefit with the help of Jesus Christ.

With these thoughts in mind, let us move on to consider the ancient precept of **firstfruits**, an aspect of giving instituted through Moses while the Israelites were in the wilderness. Ancient though it is, and related to the Law of Moses as delivered three thousand years ago, the principle it speaks of holds current and contemporary relevance.

When the Israelites finally came out of the wilderness under Joshua's leadership, the first obstacle they faced was the city of Jericho, at the entry point to their promised land of Canaan. After the remarkable series of events at Jericho recounted in Joshua 6, the Israelites prepared to do battle with the smaller neighbouring town of Ai, which, after reconnaissance, they reckoned to be easy meat. The severe casualties the Israelites suffered there came as a surprise to them, and were attributed, after investigation, to an instance of grievous sin. Joshua had said, before the Israelites took Jericho, *'The City and all that is in it are to be devoted to the LORD'* (Joshua 6:17). The footnote in my Bible says, 'The Hebrew term translated *devoted* refers to the irrevocable giving over of things or persons to the Lord, often by totally destroying them.' So Jericho, with all its inhabitants and their possessions, was put to the sword and burnt to the ground, saving only the gold, silver, bronze and iron which was put into the treasury. Why then was God so angry when a man named Achan took some of the plunder for himself? Allow me a free translation of his defence statement:

> *'In all the booty we took out from Jericho, I saw a designer suit and several thousand pounds' worth of gold and silver. I wanted them, and so I took them.'*   (Joshua 7:21)

So why the trouble? The chief issue is one of disobedience, but further to this, God insists that the first things always belong to Him. All the wealth of the rest of the land, as many clothes as Achan and his family could ever wear, would be free for them to take in future conquests, but these were the first things, and they belong to God.

I have understood this principle for a long time. My first salary as a boy of sixteen was given to the Lord's work, but in recent years this truth of 'firstfruits' has acquired a stronger meaning with me. When I see the ferocity with which God avenges disobedience to the principle in the Jericho story, it makes me think. The Bible says,

> *'Honour the Lord with your wealth, with the firstfruits of all your crops; then your barns will be filled to overflowing, and your vats will brim over with new wine.'*
>   (Proverbs 3:9–10)

When Moses legislated the principles of firstfruits, the Lord said to the Israelites,

> *'When you enter the land I am going to give you and reap its harvest, bring to the priest a sheaf of the first grain you harvest.'*
>   (Leviticus 23:10)

Firstly then, the first sheaf represents the whole as offered to God. Next, it makes the rest of the crop holy. Paul said:

> *'If the part of the dough offered as firstfruits is holy, then the whole batch is holy; if the root is holy, so are the branches.'*
>   (Romans 11:16)

Thirdly, firstfruits expresses thanks, rest and confidence in the God who has brought the first sheaf to maturity, since God, who makes things grow, will care for the rest also. As a picture of this truth, the people of Israel rested from normal work on this special day (Numbers 28:26).

I have friends with horticultural tendencies who give away the first ripe portion of the crop as a firstfruit. The rest of their allotment crops always seem to flourish, with only the occasional failure! For most of us, though, first-fruits will involve money. In the first weeks of a new year, a time we have found convenient, my wife Dorothy and I habitually bring our firstfruit gift as a holy offering to God. We are saying, 'You, Lord, have given us the energy and strength to earn this money; we want the rest of the money we receive this year to be holy also [which makes it hard to waste, but doesn't stop us enjoying it!]. We praise You today for Your faithfulness, and we rest in faith that all our needs are met and that Your blessing will provide for us to sow generously during this year.' I have proved that the principle works, as manifested in money saved, designer clothes bought at a fraction of their normal cost, days of rest and places to write (I'm in Spain as I write this) and unexpected gifts to pay for family weddings. God is true to His word.

One more amazing thought about first things. Paul identified the risen Christ as *'the firstfruits of those who have fallen asleep'* (1 Corinthians 15:20). Remember again the Jericho story: all the 'first' things were to be devoted to the Lord by destroying them, even to the point of taking life. There is also the test Abraham was put to in which God asks for his only son, Isaac. When Isaac questioned his father, *'the fire and wood are here ... but where is the lamb for the burnt offering?'* (Genesis 22:7), Abraham answered with words that I am convinced still reverberate around eternity:

> *'God Himself will provide the lamb for the burnt offering, my son.'*   (Genesis 22:8)

When the test was at an end, Abraham

> *'Saw a ram caught by its horns ... He called the place The Lord Will Provide. And to this day it is said, "On the mountain of the Lord it will be provided."'*
> (Genesis 22:13, 14)

This picture, painted in ancient history, points to the same mountain where another lamb, a human lamb, not caught in the thicket but wearing a crown of thorns, was to lay down His own life. Almighty God, living by His own rules and utterly devoting the first things, gave His only Son to die on a cross, thereby breaking the curse of sin hanging over all mankind. He was then raised up again as an offering representing all mankind, making all holy, and guaranteeing the rest of the harvest. Paul spoke of the matter thus:

> *'Each in his own turn: Christ the firstfruits; then ... those who belong to Him.'*   (1 Corinthians 15:23)

James wrote similarly,

> *'He chose to give us birth through the word of truth, that we might be a kind of firstfruits of all He created.'*
> (James 1:18)

This means that you and I are given as a firstfruit before God, representing the whole of creation, to make it holy. The kingdom fully established and the whole creation in proper order will, one day, be ready to work with the Creator into the eternity of His planning and delight. Whoopee! God believes in firstfruits, and if you want to live in the promised land, so must you.

In closing, let me ask: Are you a reaper? Then you must have been a sower! Are you a sower? Then you will be a reaper! Remember, the seed you sow corresponds directly to the harvest you reap.

'Good and Evil both increase at compound interest.'
(C.S. Lewis, *Mere Christianity*,
Fontana books, 1983 edn, p.115)

Are you in the way of offering the firstfruits of your life to God? His goodness to us is solely due to His grace, but that does not relieve us of our responsibilities to His requirements and commands. Let us look to enjoy some more 'compound interest' as every day, in every way, we thank God for 'seed for bread' and 'seed to sow'. As in the Promised Land of the Old Testament the harvest will be watered and plentiful.

Chapter 15

Let's Party!

'Being cheerful keeps you healthy; it is a slow death to be gloomy all the time.' (Proverbs 17:22, Good News Bible)

That is good advice, but to suggest that God might follow His own advice and laugh or sing, or that Jesus would ever have been filled with joy and vitality – that is preposterous, surely? I can hear the modern-day Pharisees now – in no way advertisements for dynamic Christian living – appealing through tightly pursed lips, 'But you don't understand! Jesus was a man of sorrows! The world is in a mess, people are going to hell! How dare you suggest that we should have a party?'

And so here we have another of the many apparent paradoxes which make up the Christian faith. What these people say is true: Jesus was indeed a man of deeper sorrows than we may truly comprehend, but He was also *'set by God above His companions by being anointed with the oil of joy'* (Psalm 45:7). We will consider the example of Jesus a little later, but first we must reflect upon the wider nature of God as observed throughout the Old Testament.

God reveals Himself by His names. In the opening pages of the Bible he is *Elohim* – the Creator (Genesis 1:1) – the One who made everything from nothing by His Word (even a 'word' is viewed as a 'thing' in the Hebrew language).[1]

---

[1] The Hebrew word *dabar* may be rendered *word, event, thing, commandment* or *promise* in English, depending upon the context in which it appears.

This is a demonstration of authority and power beyond the fission and fusion of atomic energy. God manifests Himself in creation as omnipotent and sovereign. So how does such an awe-inspiring, breath-taking Being make Himself available to His creation? How does He help His creation approach Him? By revealing Himself as *Jehovah*, the relational God who makes agreements, promises and covenants with His creation – specifically, with mankind. This is a God with clear emotions: love and tenderness, anger and jealousy, who talks with His friends and shares Himself with others. Even though we are so much less than Him, we are created in His image and likeness.

Good though this is, it is still not enough to satisfy this all-powerful and relational Being; He wants to help His creation, meet its needs, and be a provider. He therefore takes for Himself another name: *El-Shaddai*, the all-sufficient one (literally, the many-breasted one), the one who succours, cares for and meets the needs of His creation. You might say, 'But what's in a name?' God called Himself these and other names because He already was what the names described. The God of the Bible reveals Himself as the all-powerful, relational provider because He is who He is, always in complete command of every situation. His names describe different facets of His own nature. Each name He takes for Himself sheds light upon one or more of His various attributes.

The Psalmist frequently illuminates the breadth of God's personality:

> *'Why do the nations conspire and the peoples plot in vain? The kings of the earth take their stand and the rulers gather together against the Lord ... [But] the one enthroned in heaven laughs; The Lord scoffs at them. Then He rebukes them in His anger and terrifies them with His wrath.'*
>
> (Psalm 2:1–5)

He is clearly very secure in His absolute sovereignty. Due to His love of harmony, He rejoices when relationships are good.

'When brothers live together in unity ... the Lord bestows
His blessing.' (Psalm 133:1, 3)

Because of His generous and caring nature, He is fulfilled
when He provides for our needs.

'As a father has compassion on his children, so the Lord has
compassion on those who fear Him; for He knows how we
are formed, He remembers that we are dust.'
(Psalm 103:13, 14)

Zephaniah delivers another distinctive insight regarding
the whole nature of God. Having warned the countries to
which he spoke, he foresaw God's mercy and therefore
encouraged his audience to sing, shout, be glad and rejoice,
because

'The Lord your God is with you, He is mighty to save. He
will take great delight in you, He will quiet you with His
love, He will rejoice over you with singing.'
(Zephaniah 3:17)

It would be a shame to miss such a party!

While the Israelites were in the desert, preparing to enter
their Promised Land, God gave them various command-
ments relating to a diverse range of matters. Obedience to
these instructions would, He said, benefit every area of their
lives. Within the directives they received were some specific
instructions about feast days (Leviticus 23). Firstly they
were to have a day of rest from work every week, the
Sabbath, on which a sacred assembly would be held. Then
there were several main celebrations to be recognised each
year. During the first month, the Passover was to be
celebrated, followed by the Feast of Weeks (Pentecost) fifty
days later. In the seventh month they enjoyed the Feast of
Trumpets and the Feast of Tabernacles. Once the harvest
was gathered in, God gave the order to celebrate. The text of
the Bible suggests a time of eating, resting and remembering
God's faithfulness.

'So beginning with the fifteenth day of the seventh month,
after you have gathered the crops of the land, celebrate the

*festival to the Lord for seven days; the first day is a day of
rest, and the eighth day also is a day of rest. On the first day
you are to take choice fruit from the trees, and palm fronds,
leafy branches and poplars, and rejoice before the Lord your
God for seven days. Celebrate this as a festival to the Lord
for seven days each year.'*   (Leviticus 23:39–41)

Clearly, it was not God's desire to crush His people, or
lock them into grinding servitude. He required that they
remember Him and His saving help, but for the main part in
an atmosphere of joy and celebration. This is a very
different picture to that which some Christians portray!

Turning from the basic nature of God and the celebrations that He instituted, let us look now at the life of Jesus.
Observing His remarkably balanced character through the
history presented in the Gospels, we see a man who could
be happy, weep, tell stories or be very serious. He could
enjoy a feast or go away alone to pray. He was a wonderful
human being who manifested the whole range of human
emotions, and possessed an undeniably magnetic personality. Jesus was indeed a man of sorrows, but He was also a
man of exuberance and *joie de vivre* beyond that of other
men.

Consider Jesus' first recorded miracle, which occurred at a
wedding – not during a week of prayer. Jesus turned over
500 litres of water into the best wine anyone tasted that
day. This must have made for a happy feast! I have friends
who for conscience' sake, or because of the misuse of
alcohol, abstain from drinking, and I honour them; but I
find it difficult to stomach sanctimonious legalists who
argue that the wine mentioned in the Bible was not wine
but unfermented grape juice. There is also the bizarre
suggestion that the wine Paul instructed Timothy to take
'because of your stomach' (1 Timothy 5:23) was administered
in medicinal, teaspoon quantities! Certainly, God hates
drunkenness along with every other form of abuse and
excess – He calls us to be self-controlled. But I can't help
thinking that many Christians would be found sitting in
the corner complaining, had they been with Jesus at the

wedding. The misunderstanding of the paradox that the *'man of sorrows'* is the same person as the man *'anointed with the oil of joy'* is a deep-rooted one.

It is our lot to both be grave about the serious state of our world, and to enjoy the time God has given us. This is the tension: we are not to

> *'Think of ourselves more highly than we ought, but rather think of ourselves with sober judgement, in accordance with the measure of faith God has given us.'*   (Romans 12:3)

Yet God has decided that through us, His Church, He will cause His Kingdom to be established. So let us not take ourselves too seriously but be able to laugh at ourselves, while never relinquishing our responsibility of crying out for our lost world.

Jesus Himself had to find the correct balance between celebration and seriousness. In response to the accusatory thoughts of the Pharisees, Jesus replied,

> *'John the Baptist came neither eating bread nor drinking wine, and you say, "He has a demon." The son of man came eating and drinking, and you say, "Here is a glutton and a drunkard, a friend of tax collectors and sinners." But wisdom is proved right by all her children.'*
>
> (Luke 7:33–35)

This is the wisdom we require: to know the right way to behave at the right time. To a man of ill repute, Jesus said easily and simply without show or fuss, *'Zacchaeus, ... I must stay at your house today'* (Luke 19:5). Jesus was entirely unconcerned about guilt by association: He went modestly about His Father's business, teaching, preaching, healing, helping, and touching the physically, socially and morally untouchable. *'It is not the healthy who need a doctor, but the sick,'* (Luke 5:31) He said. Wherever He found them, of good or bad reputation, He helped them – often in a relaxed atmosphere of food, drink and celebrations.

As the time of Jesus' suffering and death approached, and in consequence of His remarkable miracles, *'a dinner was given in Jesus' honour'* (John 12:2). At the meal, a lady named

Mary poured a large quantity of very valuable perfume over Jesus' feet. The Gospel accounts of this event (Matthew 26:6–13; Mark 14:3–9; John 12:1–8) record the variety of responses which Mary's action elicited. Some – most notably the disciples – were scandalised because they knew the value of the perfume, and began criticising Mary for her extravagant gesture. They considered her extravagance to be utterly wasteful. Extravagance does not always equate to waste, but many people are trapped by that opinion. We must learn that on some occasions, extravagance is entirely appropriate: this sounds both dangerous and exciting!

Please grasp something of the spirit in which I have written this chapter. Many Christians, including myself, have been brought up with a serious understanding of duty and responsibility. We must be good stewards of our time and resources, and treasure them both, taking care not to waste anything. We have received this model from a wide range of very different traditions – the asceticism of the desert Fathers, a form of stoicism from the Greeks; the work ethic of the reformation generations; Wesley's motto, 'Earn all you can, save all you can, give all you can'. All these influences, among many others, have shaped for us the serious, sober side of being a Christian. We may need to redress the balance by recalling that the God of the Bible and His Son, Jesus Christ, both know how to laugh, have instituted celebration as part of human existence, and strongly desire to enjoy our lives with us. Cultivation of a cheerful attitude is not solely for the benefit of those around you, either: the words with which I opened this chapter are medically sound. It is a well-accredited observation that those who are cheerful tend to be healthier. As I said at the beginning of this chapter, quoting from a different version of the Bible,

> 'A cheerful heart is good medicine, but a crushed spirit dries up the bones.'   (Proverbs 17:22)

This is the physical significance behind Nehemiah's counsel to the Israelites:

'The joy of the Lord is your strength.'   (Nehemiah 8:10)

The Israelites in the wilderness had to learn the various meanings of the sound of trumpets (Numbers 10:1–10). Sometimes they summoned the leaders to gather; at other times, the whole nation were to assemble. The trumpets sounded when it was time to move forward into new territory, or when it was time to go to war. They also sounded to tell the nation that it was time for a festival, a celebration, or a party. We also must learn to discern the times, so that we may act appropriately at the correct time. We will be healthier, happier – and, I suspect, holier – if we learn to celebrate as a part of our pilgrimage too. It will make the road through the promised land an easier one to travel.

Chapter 16

A Look at the Opposition

It's an invasion! The whole place is being overrun! If we have ants in the kitchen or a wasps' nest in the eaves, we may need to clear away whatever is attracting them, and consider using some insecticide. If the neighbourhood is suffering a crime wave, we should take steps for better security and perhaps fit some new locks to our doors and windows. If our country were facing an aggressive army, new locks or pest control chemicals would not figure high on the list of priorities. Knowing something about the opposition is always information of great value.

In Numbers 13 and 14 we read the account of the time Moses sent some spies to explore Canaan. Intimidated by the inhabitants of the land, ten of the twelve explorers spread a bad report among their countrymen. Yes, it was a fruitful land with many attractive possibilities, but

> *'The people who live there are powerful, and the cities are fortified and very large. We even saw giants there ... We can't attack those people; they are stronger than we are ... The land we explored devours those living in it. All the people we saw there are of great size ... We seemed like grasshoppers in our own eyes and we looked the same to them.'* (Numbers 13:28–33)

How did they know what they looked like to the people of the land? Had they stopped to ask them? The majority won the day, even though Joshua and Caleb said *'We should go up and take possession of the land, for we can certainly do it'* (13:30). The invasion was postponed forty years as a consequence.

How often the majority are wrong. That one tragic decision caused a whole generation of people to miss their potential. They died in the wilderness instead of drinking wine in the Promised Land because they mis-read the strength of the opposition. Once the forty years had passed, the true situation became apparent when some different spies spoke to one of the inhabitants of the land, who said,

> *'I know that the Lord has given this land to you and that a great fear of you has fallen on us, so that all who live in this country are melting in fear because of you.'*   (Joshua 2:9)

I am sure the Lord had put the same fear in the Canaanites a generation earlier, but most of the spies failed to see it. Many Christians live in fear of what the devil can do to them, when the clear teaching of Paul indicates that the reverse is true.

> *'He stripped all the spiritual tyrants in the universe of their sham authority at the Cross and marched them naked through the streets.'*   (Colossians 2:15, *The Message*)

Treat your enemy with proper wariness by all means – to do anything less is folly – but never credit him with more power or authority than he actually has.

So, there are giants in the land. Regarding the 'fight of right against might' in the story of David and Goliath (1 Samuel 17), some may have said (in confidence or bluster), 'He's too big to miss.' Others may have been cautious or nervous and said, 'He's too strong to fail', and been intimidated. David took a different tack entirely:

> *'I come against you in the name of the Lord Almighty ... This day the Lord will hand you over to me.'*
> (1 Samuel 17:45, 46)

This approach is all very well, but what are our giants?

Joshua's people had some tall enemies, but beyond the physical challenge, they really needed to think a different way – your mind is your business, as we have already seen.

They also needed to learn to live a different way. The Bible tells us that by giving we receive, by dying we live, by humbling ourselves we are lifted up. This is a very unusual lifestyle when compared to the tactic promoted by most cultures around the world: 'survival of the fittest' or 'look after number one.' After forty years of this policy in the wilderness, a different strategy was required whereby whole tribes had to co-operate with one another to gain their inheritances. The Church, divided into its many denominational tribes, has much to learn about the degree of togetherness required for it to triumph in some of the battles that face it.

We must each avail ourselves of the power and strength of God if we are to prevail against our individual problems, our personal giants. Having proved God in the daily routines of life and the challenges they present, we will gain greater courage and confidence to join together and drive the bigger giants out of our land. All the key people involved in taking the Promised Land had to learn the same lesson. Joshua was commanded by God to *'be strong and very courageous'* (Joshua 1:7). Caleb was still resolute after more than forty years of waiting to personally succeed and enjoy his inheritance. The lesson may be hard to learn, but the rewards it offers are invaluable.

What wider issues should we consider about our opposition? Insight into the enemy's tactics is priceless. We will consider four. First, any enemy will enjoy where possible the anonymity provided by camouflage – being hidden, deceiving. The Bible says that the Devil sometimes appears as an angel of light. Many evangelical Christians have a comfortable theology that leaves the demonic world hidden under its camouflage and therefore more insidiously effective. The message of some extremists may be an unhelpful exaggeration, but wild over-emphasis should not be allowed to blind us to the truth. There is widespread ignorance and indifference (in some cases, outright opposition) to the use of the gift of discerning of sprits. The need for this, as part of our Kingdom mandate to cast out demons, is vital if people are to be released from desperate situations. I include Christians on their pilgrim journey, some of whom need to be released from demonic power and activity themselves.

A second key tactic involves demoralising one's opponents. In war, armies will employ any sabotage in order to weaken the resolve of their enemies. One of the most effective means is the continual bombardment of one's opponents' position. In 1900, the Christian religion was predominantly a Western faith. At the turn of the millennium, the picture is reversed in a truly remarkable demographic shift. Throughout the twentieth century the Church experienced dramatic growth throughout the developing world, while the slumbering Western Church is in need of Isaiah's call to 'Awake'. Battered from within and without by its sense of failure, decline and insecurity, it is an easy target to hammer with the views of science and philosophy, which have combined to expose the Western Church's uncertainty in her message and role in the world.

It is hard to reconcile this fatigued shadow with the Church in the rest of the world or the one spoken of in the New Testament.

> '[God's] *intent was that now, through the church, the manifold wisdom of God should be made known to the rulers and authorities in the heavenly realms.'* (Ephesians 3:10)

For what reason is the Western Church so cautious? Why does it lack the vibrancy and dynamism of its New Testament counterparts and that of its contemporaries in Asia, Africa and throughout Central and Southern America? The reason is that an enemy has demoralised too many of us. It is time to get busy with our true agenda and stop listening to the lies of this so called post-Christian age, and take our promised land by living to God's purpose, asking God for His mercy on our prosperous but indifferent people.

A third tactic in warfare is the use of distraction. Depending on its equipment, training and ability in any given terrain, an army will either display its strength or expose its weakness. The rigours of war, the ability of leaders to co-ordinate the various specialist units, and a host of tactical requirements all play their part in determining the eventual outcome. Any good army will attempt to fight on its point of strength. A battle may turn if one side is distracted. How have we been susceptible to distraction?

The Western Church has allowed itself to be out-manoeuvred, leaving it in a weakened position. The ordination of women and the Church's response to homosexuality are important issues, but should they have been allowed to dominate the agenda to the degree they have done in recent years? The Church has often been slow to speak out on matters relating to global or ethical responsibility, shy of insisting that the confession of Christianity carries with it explicit standards of behaviour for all people, individually and corporately. In New Testament times, the Church fared better, preaching a strong, radical, life-changing message – in short, fulfilling its God-given mandate. Even through the fires of persecution, it turned the world upside down. As we attend to our prime responsibility once again, the Church will succeed in its task, and the secondary issues will find their proper place.

The fourth matter we will consider is that of weaponry. Armies clamour for new and better equipment; faster, more versatile aeroplanes; heavier guns; better surveillance. Paul explained,

> *'The world is unprincipled. It's dog-eat-dog out there! The world doesn't fight fair. But we don't fight our battles that way – never have and never will. The tools of our trade aren't for marketing or manipulation, but they are for demolishing that entire massively corrupt culture. We use our powerful God-tools for smashing warped philosophies, tearing down barriers erected against the truth of God, fitting every loose thought and emotion into the structure of life shaped by Christ. Our tools are ready for clearing the ground of every obstruction and building lives of obedience and maturity.'*
>
> (2 Corinthians 10:3–6, *The Message*)

There is to me no conflict in the use of modern technology, with better public relations and modern methods for promotion of our message, but its employment in competition with the spirit of the age is a great folly. Our reliance must remain in the power and principles of the Gospel.

The right use of our minds is important, but the debate is much wider here. The deep arguments developed in dark minds and quietly propagated in university lecture halls during the nineteenth and twentieth centuries have stolen up on us. They have raped truth and virtue, substituting them for relativism and an arbitrary value system. The Church has a job to do and strongholds to tear down. It has a rising generation of students and intellectuals which it must educate with different arguments – people with minds developed, enlightened and inspired by the Holy Spirit. Anything less will leave a grim legacy to surviving generations.

Michael Novak has expressed this with more clarity than most. Having remarked that 'in the 20th century, prisons and torture chambers have been better places to encounter God than universities,' he goes on to observe:

'Vulgar relativism is an invisible gas, odourless, deadly, that is now polluting every society on earth. It is a gas that attacks the central nervous system of moral striving. This most perilous threat to the free society today is neither political nor economic. It is the poisonous, corrupting culture of relativism ... Freedom requires the exercise of conscience ... During the past 100 years, the question for those who loved liberty was whether, relying on the virtues of our peoples, we could survive the most powerful assaults from without. During the next 100 years, the question for those who love liberty is whether we can survive the most insidious and duplicitous attacks from within, from those that undermine the virtues of our people, doing in advance the work of the Father of Lies. "There is no such thing as truth," they teach even the little ones. "Truth is bondage. Believe what seems right to you. There are as many truths as there are individuals. Follow your feelings. Do as you please. Get in touch with yourself.

Do what feels comfortable." This is how they speak, those who prepare the jails of the 21st century. Those who undermine the idea of truth do the work of tyrants.'   (Michael Novak, Templeton Prize Lecture)

An old English hymn says, 'Christians arise and put your armour on, clothed in the strength of Christ alone.' The Bible urges each of us to fight the fight of faith. How are we to fight? There are giants in the land, but what are they and how are we to fight them?

Some are giants of the mind – the 'grasshopper' attitude of blinded minds, the inability to identify opposition and deadly unbelief. Some are giants of inactivity. Many do not heed the injunction to fight, refusing to use our democratic and God-provided opportunities of protest, thereby missing far better alternatives and accepting a too compliant, sometimes apathetic stance. They somehow believe that God will work everything out, when in fact biblical and contemporary history show that His plan is to use people like you and me to further His purposes, bringing change for the betterment of society. Surely we must grasp the operation of the salt and light principle, and the necessity to understand the demanding words of Jesus that:

> *'Until now the kingdom of heaven has been forcefully advancing and forceful men lay hold of it,'*
> (Matthew 11:12)

or the equally challenging concept expressed by Christ in the next chapter:

> *'How can anyone enter a strong man's house and carry off his possessions unless he first ties up the strong man?'*
> (Matthew 12:29)

Oh, there are many giants in the land. It was true for the children of Israel entering their Promised Land, and it was true for David facing his Goliath. Nothing changes. People and families, communities, churches, districts and nations – they all have giants which must be dealt with. These giants may be obstacles to 'pilgrims', objections to principles,

obvious weaknesses that limit progress, or disguised inter-
ruptions and inconveniences, but each and every giant is an
opportunity to take more of our promised land. A friend of
mine suffered from a speech impediment, but he loved the
Bible and wanted to speak about its truth. The problem was
a giant standing between him and part of his promised
land. He eventually killed his giant and reached his
potential. Then there was the barren woman who broke
through in her faith and enjoyed the 'impossible' birth
of a child, while another lovely Christian woman I met
recently triumphed against her disappointment in child-
lessness.

Let's think again about David and Goliath – the story of
the perceived underdog emerging victorious is one to be
relished. This anointed young man was an obedient, disciplined and successful son of an honourable father who had
proved that God will and can help in times of need.

He had confidence in the God who had helped him in
times past, and trusted in God's continued commitment to
him. When Goliath roared with aggression and threats,
David said, *'I come against you in the name of the Lord
Almighty'* (1 Samuel 17:45). He didn't seek simply to influence his enemy or to bind and limit his power; he removed
him in a decisive victory.

David had selected five stones: the first one removed his
giant, but what of the other four? Legend has it that they
served a similar purpose against the giant's brothers! It's a
nice idea. If you were given five stones and told to perform a
similar task to David – remove five giants that were hinder-
ing the life of your nation – what would you choose to see
destroyed?

In our lives, individually, as part of a local community of
Christians and as part of the universal Church of Jesus
Christ, let us rise up like David and kill our giants, for God
has given us mightier weapons than stones and slings.

> *'The weapons we fight with are not the weapons of the
> world. On the contrary, they have divine power to demolish
> strongholds. We demolish arguments and every pretension*

> *that sets itself up against the knowledge of God, and we take*
> *captive every thought to make it obedient to Christ...'*
>
> (2 Corinthians 10:4–5)

Who knows, in our day we may yet see our country dramatically changed. Even Britain's many grim moral and spiritual facets can be altered beyond recognition. In David's day, they ended up dancing in the streets. We may receive the same joy when our country is similarly transformed. With God's help I intend to use my five stones wisely. What will you do with yours?

Having looked at the opposition and faced the challenge of the need to fight, what other principles must we examine if we are to successfully live in our promised land?

Before concluding his message to the Ephesian church, Paul expressed very strongly that:

> *'Our struggle is not against flesh and blood* [I wish more Christians would remember that fact], *but against the rulers, against the authorities, against the power of this dark world and against the spiritual forces of evil in the heavenly realms.'*   (Ephesians 6:12)

He then provided much good advice about behaviour, battle dress, weapons, prayer, and persistence. When you have done everything else – stand. When you trip, falter or fall – stand again. What can help us to keep standing? Look again at the famous war story in 2 Chronicles 20:1–30, I can see seven points on which to stand:

1. **Stand in prayer** (v. 5–6). *'Jehoshaphat stood up ... and said, "O Lord ... "'*

2. **Stand in agreement** (v. 13). *'All the men ... with their wives, children and little ones stood there before the Lord.'*

3. **Stand on prophecy** (v. 14–16). *'...as he stood ... he said ... do not be afraid or discouraged.'*

4. **Stand in worship** (v. 18). *'After standing they bowed and fell down in worship.'*

5. **Stand in praise** (v. 19). *'The priests ... stood up and praised the Lord ... with a very loud voice.'*

6. **Stand in song** (v. 21). *'Coming out of their worship and praise the king appointed men to sing to the Lord . . . as they went out at the head of the army.'*

7. **Stand in victory** (v. 2–30). *'The Lord set ambushes, and they enjoyed a great victory with much spoils.'*

When we take our position and stand firm on the promises given by God, consistent practice of the above disciplines will eventually lead to a victory.

I find the story in John 11 of Lazarus being raised from the dead fascinating, not least because of the timing. Jesus waited a long time before even starting His journey to face the problem. It was a longer wait for the two distraught sisters. What should we do when we have 'eyeballed' the opposition, maintained the fight, held our ground by standing firm, and still we don't see the victory? We must learn to **wait**. We are not usually good at waiting and can impetuously do the wrong thing simply through our inability to be patient. Here are a few do's and don'ts that have helped me to wait during the times of frustration:

*   **Don't** ask unnecessary questions or dream wistful 'if only' scenarios.

*   Face the facts, like Abraham in Romans 4:19, but **don't** trust human logic.

*   **Do** continue to believe – a key word in the John 11 story of Lazarus – *'so that you may believe'* (v. 15); *'Do you believe this?'* (v. 26); *'Did I not tell you that if you believed, you would see the glory of God?'* (v. 40).

*   **Do** maintain your confession of the Lordship of Jesus, even in your doubts. *'Lord, if you had been here, my brother would not have died'* (v. 32).

*   **Do** maintain your obedience – *'Whatever He says, do it.'*

We know we have opposition, but suitable weapons are available. We are learning how to **stand** and if necessary **wait**, so let us refocus and take aim again.

We are not to be demoralized, imagining ourselves to have the stature of grasshoppers; our enemies know (and we do well to remind both them and ourselves) that the one who is in us is greater than the one who is in the world (1 John 4:4). The words of Jesus ring throughout the Church:

'Take heart! I have overcome the world.' (John 16:33)

Wherever the opposition chooses to fight, whatever false philosophy is propounded, the morale of the forces of light remains high. Our purpose is clear, so let us fill our vision with the certainty of the promises of God.

Chapter 17

Comin' in on a Wing
and a Prayer

You may have read books that teach about prayer, or tell the histories of some of the world's 'prayer warriors'. Some contain inspiring and oft-repeated quotations, or detail the incredible faith of people in far-flung lands. Sometimes I'm motivated by such books; by others, I'm left breathless and weak at the knees. Effective prayer is an integral part of attaining our promised land lifestyle, and so we must seek to study and develop our ability to pray. Here, however, there will be no famous quotations, and no intimidating tales from history's saints. Rather, let us take a pilgrim's look at the example Jesus sets us in the Gospels, that we ourselves might aspire to be men and women of prayer. Reading the accounts of Jesus' life, I see a man who prayed not from a sense of ritual duty, nor to maintain a stoic discipline, but one who delighted in continual communion with His Father. At times He seems almost formal, at others less so, but there is always reality. This unceasing intimacy with God is the goal we seek.

Observe a couple of events in Jesus' life which emphasise an important facet of His character. When His anxious parents found their twelve-year-old son after He had been missing for three days, the defence He offered was,

'Didn't you know I had to be in my fathers house?'

(Luke 2:49)

Eighteen years later, after His baptism and temptation in the wilderness,

> *'He went to Nazareth, where He had been brought up, and on the Sabbath day He went into the synagogue, as was His custom.'*   (Luke 4:16)

Two seemingly unrelated incidents, but it is reasonable for us to conclude from them that Jesus' inward life of fellowship with His Father was reinforced by His regular attendance at the synagogue. In the fifty plus years of my life I have been helped in prayer by consistent attendance at a place of worship. The spiritual state of Christians who care little for regular and disciplined fellowship with others is always a cause for concern.

Once Jesus' ministry was in full swing, people were being healed, evil spirits were being driven out, and Jesus was calling His disciples – but what about prayer? The number of references to Jesus' prayer life are surprisingly limited. Matthew recounts Jesus' teaching on prayer in chapter 6, but we reach chapter 11 before we read His public offering of praise to His Father. Not until chapter 14 do we read the first formal statement of Jesus' personal prayer experience:

> *'He went up on a mountainside by Himself to pray.'*
> (Matthew 14:23)

Mark tells us,

> *'Very early in the morning, while it was still dark, Jesus got up, left the house and went off to a solitary place, where He prayed.'*   (Mark 1:35)

Luke is even briefer:

> *'At daybreak Jesus went out to a solitary place.'*
> (Luke 4:42)

Luke does inform us though, that:

> *'Jesus often withdrew to lonely places and prayed.'*
> (Luke 5:16)

Do the few references to Jesus' prayer life suggest that prayer is unimportant? I would conclude the opposite: Jesus' early morning practice of spending time alone with His Father was such a fundamental part of His routine that it is not frequently mentioned. Jesus lived His life on earth in continuous communion with God, and out of that relationship made all His decisions. The appointing of the twelve apostles came in such a way. We would do well to make our choices in an atmosphere of prayer, listening to hear God's heart.

Jesus shared a key secret with His disciples on one occasion:

> *'I do exactly what my Father has commanded me.'*
> (John 14:31)

How the command was communicated to Him is not disclosed. Did the Father take Him through the events of the day during their early morning times together, or did those times produce such a closeness that, at a moment's notice, He had the 'inner witness' and certainty of what should happen next? I have a hunch it was a combination of the two. Jesus' earlier words provide support for this hunch:

> *'The Son ... can do only what He sees His Father doing, because whatever the Father does the Son also does. For the Father loves the Son and shows Him all He does.'*
> (John 5:19, 20)

Personally speaking, I have often been amazed to hear myself speaking the right words or finding myself in the right place. The stronger my intimacy with God, the easier it is to be effective and fulfilled. Recall the healing of the sick woman:

> *' "Who touched me?" Jesus asked. Peter said, "Master, the people are crowding and pressing against you." But Jesus said, "Someone touched me; I know that power has gone out from me." '*
> (Luke 8:45, 46)

A question I'm more interested in hearing the answer to is, 'How did the power get into Jesus in the first place?' During His ministry, thousands of people were healed and delivered from demons. Some were raised from the dead. John tells us the scope of amazing events that were an integral part of the life and times of Jesus Christ:

> *'Jesus did many other things as well. If every one of them were written down, I suppose that even the whole word would not have room for the books that would be written.'*
> (John 21:25)

Where did all that virtue come from? Jesus laid aside all the advantages of His 'God-ness' and lived and triumphed as a human being. Always being filled with the Holy Spirit, His ongoing relationship and intimacy with God must have contributed hugely to His stamina and vitality, allowing healing and power to flow out of Him. This takes no account of the energy needed for simply living and travelling, or the demands of His extended teaching ministry, or the questions He was continually bombarded with. Deep within me, I know His prayer life lay at the foundation of everything He did. Jesus typically led by example. He told His disciples the parable of the persistent widow to teach them that *'they should always pray and not give up'* (Luke 18:1). On another occasion, He used the illustration of a man needing food from a friend at midnight (Luke 11:5–8). How many of us would achieve much more and reach our potential if we learned to truly persist in prayer until we attained our goal?

John's account of the resurrection of Lazarus illustrates the public side of Jesus' prayer life. Looking up to heaven He prayed aloud, expressing His certainty that His Father always heard Him. He had already prayed privately and had the answer to the present emergency, as implied by His words, *'I thank you that you have heard me'* (John 11:41). Lazarus came out of the grave and the whole family was happy again. Why did Jesus pray the way He did? He Himself gives us the answer: *'That they may believe that you sent me'* (John 11:42). It seems that there are occasions when public prayer is simply the focal point for people's faith; the harder work of petition, intercession and spiritual warfare having already been completed in private. Many Christians are able to pray the public prayers; I am not sure they have always done the more important private work. If we follow the example of Jesus and maintain our private prayer life, our public prayer life might well be more effective, and more people would believe as a consequence of hearing us pray.

Jesus' teaching brings prayer into the daily round of life. Prayer is not purely some contemplative act far removed from the realities of our ordinary world. *'Give us this day our daily bread'* (Matthew 6:11) is direct, relevant and specific to our physical needs. In His message about the future, Jesus speaks of pregnant women and nursing mothers, and counsels, *'pray that your flight will not take place in winter'* (Matthew 24:20). At its simplest level of meaning, this is remarkably practical advice. When feeding the five thousand, He gave thanks, broke the bread and fish, and had the disciples distribute them to the people. Remarkably straightforward! How many times, sitting at a table with hot (or cooling) food, sometimes with hungry children, have I endured an interminably long 'grace' or a world-encompassing prayer! I'm not sure of the value of such an exercise when a simple heartfelt 'Thank you' would suffice.

Jesus used prayer to prepare for the many dynamic passages of His life. Before calling the twelve men who were to be His closest companions in the last three years of His life, He spent the night alone in prayer. The night of His betrayal found Him busy preparing again, having taken some of His disciples along with Him for prayer support. Inexperienced at this level of intensity, they fell asleep, exhausted by sorrow. The prophetic themes in Psalm 22 depict the horrific spiritual scene of strong bulls, roaring lions, dogs and wild oxen coming in all their ferocity to tear Jesus from His purpose. No wonder His sweat fell like drops of blood. Once the spiritual victory had been gained, He was ready for the physically and emotionally demanding act of fulfilling His purpose by dying on the cross.

In closing, let us look at the astonishing prayer Jesus prayed that night. He prayed for His disciples, and *'also for those who will believe in me through their message'* (John 17:20). That includes me and, I trust, includes you. Among the many requests He made to His Father is this:

> *'Father, I want those you have given me to be with me where I am, and to see my glory, the glory you have given me because you loved me before the creation of the world.'*
>
> (John 17:24)

One day we will be wholly with Him. For the present, let us resolve that through our intimacy in prayer we will be with Him, where He is, as best we can. Without further ado, I invite you to ask Him, with me,

> *'Lord, teach us to pray.'*   (Luke 11:1)

You might – justifiably – be wondering at the curious title I chose for this chapter. It was the title of a song by Harold Adamson in 1943, derived from the contemporary comment of a war pilot speaking from a disabled plane to ground control. To seek a profound link would be absurd; it is sufficient to emphasise the high level of dependence that we must learn to place upon prayer and our intimacy with God if we are to truly enter our promised land.

Chapter 18

Living to Give

Jesus said,

> *'It is more blessed to give than to receive.'*   (Acts 20:35)

These words were not just spoken; they were lived out, they were died for, and they received their ultimate confirmation at Jesus' resurrection.

Imagine a special family occasion. Look around the group and observe the delight shown on the faces of those who are given presents. It is good to receive gifts. In the same special family occasion you have just imagined, instead of watching the joy of the receivers, notice the glowing faces of the givers as they enjoy the recipient's obvious delight. The warm glow that accompanies the memory of giving causes the blessing to last a very long time. *'It is more blessed to give...'* (Acts 20:35).

The world is full of selfishness; many people are driven by their ego, not caring who gets hurt. Jesus gave us a different principle to live by, saying,

> *'The Son of Man did not come to be served, but to serve, and to give His life a ransom for many.'*   (Matthew 20:28)

Promised land people must deal with giants and difficulties, so I am not proposing an easy option – rather the opposite. Jesus warned us,

> *'If anyone would come after me, he must deny himself and*
> *take up his cross and follow me. For whoever wants to save*
> *his life will lose it, but whoever loses his life for my sake will*
> *find it.'*   (Matthew 16:24, 25)

A life of giving – holding all things lightly – is clearly laid
out as the higher, more rewarding and fulfilling way. You
may have been raised either in a giving or a selfish environment, but being a giver or a taker is your choice. The
examples around your life may be helpful or otherwise.
Some people are more inclined to serve and give than
others. Nevertheless, affirmative action lies in the realm of
personal choice. I do not know where you would place
yourself on the giving and receiving scale, but whatever
your disposition, training or birth, each of us must make a
decision to give rather than seek to receive, because this is
part of the lifestyle of the promised land. Whether a kind
word, a helping hand in some of life's many domestic
circumstances, sharing what we have with others, training
and discipling others from the wisdom and experience of
your own life – whatever you do, live to be a giver, for you
will be blessed.

Within a financial context, I have heard it said many
times. 'I would like to give more, but . . . ' The excuse offered
may be impoverished circumstances, problem with servicing debts, or any number of financial challenges, but at its
root lies a poor understanding of the law of seedtime and
harvest. Whatever the reason, God's intended cycle of
blessing is hindered from working. We must break out
of our needs and problems. One key is through giving.
Hearing and then acting upon the secrets of generosity will
have an enormous impact on our understanding of debt.
The wilderness Israelites were instructed explicitly about
cancelling debts:

> *'Don't be hard-hearted or tight-fisted toward your poor*
> *brother.'*   (Deuteronomy 15:7)

In the mid-1970s, God spoke to us at the Christian Centre
several specific times that:

'You will lend to many nations but will borrow from none.'
(Deuteronomy 15:6 & 28:12)

At the time, we had a considerable financial debt. Through a series of miracles, combined with the generosity of the congregation, we saw that debt disappear. One of the miracles occurred as follows:

We owned some high quality printing equipment, and had been endeavouring to sell it for a year. We had a week-long water-only fast, petitioning God for His favour and provision. During the fifth day I felt prompted to study and consider the above text once again. I argued with the Spirit of God, insisting that I already knew what the verses said and understood the implications. The struggle went on for some time before I conceded. I opened my Bible to read the verses. God explained that the order of events is important: lending is the first action before 'not borrowing' can come into effect. In the context of clearing a brother's outstanding debts every seven years, 'lending' seemed like a possible euphemism for 'giving'! My conversation with God proceeded something like this:

'What do you want me to do, Lord?'

'Give the printing equipment to a Christian brother.'

'Pardon? But Lord! We're trying to sell it to help clear the debt!'

'Give, lend and you won't borrow, the Bible says.'

So, in prayer I named a man whose church needed equipment similar to that which we owned, proposing to give it to him. Within two hours we received our first enquiry in nine months regarding the printing machine, followed by a letter offering £1000 for it. After discussion with the church leadership, we agreed to honour the commitment I had made in prayer, give the equipment away, trusting God for the money we needed. Through prophecy we were encouraged that a specific debt would be cleared within one month. Ten days later we received £9000 from an unexpected source that completely cleared that debt, as prophesied. One of the keys to living free of debt lies in learning how to give.

In the mid-90s, after buying land in simple obedience to the Lord, we found ourselves challenged again about the principle we learned those years ago. A secret is to give from our resources – money, people, expertise or whatever. We are determined to keep sowing the seed. Harvest always comes. The story of how God will provide for our needs has yet to be written. But I know that a miracle will happen in our house, and I am excited to see how it unfolds. Sometimes the journey is painful and many misunderstand the test of faith. Some give up hope, others go quietly and hide. You may make mistakes; by presumption, carelessness, poor management or impatience, but the harvest will come, God's promises will become visible reality. The promised land will be possessed.

We live in a society bolstered by bank loans, credit cards and highly imaginative schemes for borrowing money. Most Western nations run deficit budgets, spending more money than they have coming in. In the face of such widespread debt, where borrowing is part of the culture, should I be worried? Is debt really a problem? Interesting questions. I posed them to a friend who has a background in business and finance. This is what he said:

The Bible clearly discourages debt. God is committed to supplying our needs, not our greed. We are told to

> *'Let no debt remain outstanding, except the continuing debt to love one another.'*   (Romans 13:8)

The reason is that debt can cause insecurity, fear and tension in the home, and even death by way of murder or suicide. Debt is easy to get into, but very difficult to get out of, not least because compound interest is always working against you. Furthermore, debt presumes upon the future (James 4:13–17). It makes the debtor a 'slave' to the lender (Proverbs 22:7).

What a scary thought. Anxiety, added pressure, and longer work hours to earn more money, all make for stress. Living in this way moves us back toward the slave mentality rather than forward into promised land provision. Only in this place of blessing can we live to give rather than struggle to survive.

The New Testament teaches that a man is a slave to whatever has mastered him (2 Peter 2:19). As mentioned above,

> *'The borrower is servant to the lender.'*   (Proverbs 22:7)

We later read,

> *'Do not be a man who strikes hands on a pledge or puts up security for debts.'*   (Proverbs 22:26)

The reason for this is that the Israelites were to be so blessed by God that borrowing would not need to be part of their life. The Gospel of Jesus offers us nothing less, freeing us from any form of slavery. Yet as noted, debt makes slaves of many people. Not only do people become slaves to debt, but their debts are negative 'seed', for:

> 'Everything produces after its kind, and the seed is in itself. It works that way in everything. The seed of strife is in strife itself. If you get into strife with someone, it will create more strife. If you give love, you can reap love. The seed is in itself.'
>
> (Charles Capps, *Seedtime and Harvest*,
> Harrison House)

Does this imply that the seed of debt is in debt? I think so. Consider how debt reproduces itself through interest rates. If we want a different harvest, we must stop sowing the seeds of further debt now. Recall the journey described in the book of Exodus. The people were slaves, dominated by their enemies. They did not immediately reach their promised land (a place that included the principle of lending and not borrowing). They first had a period of survival and dependency before their full freedom. If you are to leave the slavery of debt, your journey will probably be similar. The tough decision must be made not to sow any more debt seed by contracting further debt. For most people, a cut in expenditure to the minimum is the next necessary step.

Freedom will come. If you are in any difficulty, ask for help. Find a good Independent Financial Advisor and move toward a different way of living.

When the events of a person's life are pleasant, bills are paid, relationships are good and their work secure, things seem to go better. In debt, relationships can suffer tension, health may deteriorate, and things seem to go from bad to worse. The Bible is very straightforward about the situation. Moses said,

> *'I have set before you life and death, blessings and curses.*
> *Now choose life.'*   (Deuteronomy 30:19)

In becoming a curse for us at the cross (Deuteronomy 21:23; Galatians 3:13), Jesus has made it possible for the power of every curse over our lives to be broken. Balaam the sorcerer, hired to curse the Israelites at the edge of the promised land, had to conclude,

> *'How can I curse those whom God has not cursed? ... He*
> *has blessed, and I cannot change it.'*   (Numbers 23:8, 20)

Through Christ, God has abundantly blessed us. We can choose to live under His blessing – following the godly principles that lead to the promised land. It is a poor choice to stay 'under a curse' by disobeying God's injunctions.

Debt is a curse that can bring misery. The problem must be understood and you must **desire** to get out of it. Getting out of debt will require knowledge, patience and discipline. There is no 'quick fix'. My financial friend suggested the following key points:

- Budget carefully.
- Be honest with creditors.
- Clear small amounts to reduce the number of debt accounts.
- Use windfalls to clear debt.
- Be wise in selling assets.
- Seek wise spiritual counsel and support.
- Exercise self-control.

- Couples should recognise the man's responsibility in overseeing (not necessarily managing) the finances.
- Never go to a loan shark.
- Do not be terrified by adversity.

Many people have broken the cycle of debt in their lives and over their families. I recently met a man who had been unemployed for some years. Through a variety of circumstances he had become ensnared in £16,000 of debt. He realised the need for things to change, and his first step was obedience to God in his giving. After he began paying his tithes, his position slowly improved. Three years later, he has now found work and is free of all debt. This is not an exceptional story, but it highlights four ingredients for success against debt: a commitment to change; a commitment to give; a commitment to persevere through the 'survival' time; and principally, a belief in the faithfulness of God to break the curse of debt and poverty.

Once out of debt, how should we maintain our vigilance against it? When on the threshold of entering a commitment which will take you into debt, ask yourself, 'Will this bring me closer to my goals? Does it make financial sense? Is it essential? What will happen if I don't buy this thing?' Prepare yourself against debt by good management. Give to God and to others, and be sure to maintain your correct financial priorities. Seek first the kingdom of God, and stay close to Him. The worry and anxiety that debt brings is a health hazard, it limits your ability to give, and leaves you less in control of your affairs than is desirable. Remember that we are making a journey, driving out giants, possessing our promised land. Sometimes progress is made little by little, but stay encouraged, especially if debt has been, or currently is, a problem for you. God is on your side and offers you His help.

This chapter opened with the demanding words of Jesus, *'It is more blessed to give than receive.'* Most of us have ample evidence of the pleasure and blessedness of receiving. This fact is implied in the text. Not everyone has realised the much greater joy, pleasure and blessing of being a giver.

I have spoken about debt because it is a widespread problem and breaking free from it is a necessary step to the full enjoyment of living as a giver in your promised land. However, a poverty mind-set, which has nothing to do with the resources available, is another hindrance to the joy of giving. As a man thinks so he is. The poverty mind-set finds it extremely difficult to live generously, not only in money matters, but in the wider issues of life – the giving of time, praise, support, love: the whole round of daily living.

Many people think that limited resources are also a problem. What a great mistake! When Jesus spoke about the widow giving her tiny offering it was not measured in pounds and pence or dollars and cents, it was her extravagance that was notable! My life has been touched many times by loving simple acts of thoughtfulness that had little to do with resources. If you have allowed yourself to be trapped by such 'limited resource' thinking, break out of it and slay the giant. Begin to give out of what little you have instead of dreaming about what you would do if you had more. Almost certainly, in a little while you will enjoy more resources and your pleasure will continue to increase as you learn to be more generous. It becomes a blessed cycle. God says He is no man's debtor. He also says, whoever lends to the poor gives to God. He is watching over His own Word to perform it. Press on to greater blessing remembering the secret that

'It is more blessed to give than to receive.'

Epilogue

The Service Station

The journey isn't over but my writing has run its course. Just like embarking on any long journey, you must take breaks and rest, because possessing your promised land is a lifetime's work. Maybe such a service station is just approaching on the motorway of your life right now. Time to refuel and stretch tired limbs. Take a moment to be thankful that you have got this far, and to reflect on the beauty you have enjoyed, the frustration over delays that are happily behind you, the near-misses that thankfully stayed that way. Stop in a moment as I finish, and then travel through the ideas we have shared. Whether you had a good start in life, like me, or a tough start like my friend Mike, the power that propelled Jesus through every difficulty is more available than you or I can imagine. Coming out of a slave and survival mentality as the Israelites did is not an easy task, but, how worthwhile it promises to be; moving into the promised land with its many changes, blessings, and giants too. There are so many lessons to learn, and if you are like me, to re-learn. I am not at the end of my journey, but I have possessed enough of my promised land to know it is worth every bit of effort, changed thinking, fighting, resting, laughing, praying, giving, and everything else.

My prayer is that some of my words and ideas will inspire, challenge and focus your own journey. Thankfully there is no copyright on revelation; you are welcome to share any insights or questions you have with me at the address provided at the close of the book. If you have been helped, think about giving a copy of the book to a friend. It will be a seed sown. If you have been encouraged, I would be encouraged to hear from you. I find encouragement a great stimulus. Whatever else you do, please apply the truth. It will help you possess your unique, God-given, special **promised land**. For remember, you were **born to win** and **designed** for a happy ending.

David Shearman can be contacted
at the following address:

David Shearman
Christian Centre
104 Talbot Street
Nottingham
NG1 5GL

We hope you enjoyed reading this New Wine book.
For details of other New Wine books
and a wide range of titles from other
Word and Spirit publishers visit our website:
www.newwineministries.co.uk
email: newwine@xalt.co.uk